CHANGED

TRUE STORIES OF

FINDING GOD THROUGH

CHRISTIAN MUSIC

THE POWER OF
CHRISTIAN MUSIC™

Published by Standard Publishing, Cincinnati, Ohio. A division of Standex International Corporation. Printed in the United States of America.

Cover and interior design by Rule29.
Copyediting by Nancy B. Gibbs.
Typesetting by Peggy Theile.

ISBN 0-7847-1527-0

11 10 09 08 07 06 05   9 8 7 6 5 4 3 2 1

CHANGED

TRUE STORIES OF
FINDING GOD THROUGH
CHRISTIAN MUSIC

THE POWER OF
CHRISTIAN MUSIC™

// CHRISTY BARRITT & GINNY MCCABE //

Standard
PUBLISHING
Bringing The Word to Life™

/// TABLE OF CONTENTS ///

CHRISTY'S STORY

will never forget the week of summer camp when I was fourteen. On the final night, the campfire speaker challenged my friends and me to listen to Christian music. Something about the speaker's words stirred my interest. That night I made a decision. With the fire crackling and stars twinkling overhead, I vowed to give Christian music a try.

After I returned home, I visited the only Christian bookstore in the area. I found a small selection of music and purchased two tapes. As I familiarized myself with Amy Grant and Michael W. Smith songs, I realized Christian music was enjoyable. The tunes were catchy, and the lyrics were clean.

Shortly after, I began playing the guitar. I was determined I would be the next Amy Grant. I learned to play her song "Father's Eyes." I played it for anyone and everyone who would listen. My not-yet-developed voice and my off-rhythm strumming were applauded by all. I just knew I was on my way.

As I grew older, however, I realized God had a different plan for my life. Even though I wouldn't be the next Amy Grant I felt God's calling to write about Christian music.

Today, I am a writer and a worship leader. I continue to play occasionally at coffeehouses and concerts, but I no longer have the aspirations of being on stage for a living. I believe more strongly today than ever before that God's power can be found in Christian music and that he speaks to us through the lyrics.

Christian songs have since been a great part of my life. My friends and I vowed to never lose touch while, after our graduation exercises, "Friends Are Friends Forever" by Michael W. Smith played in the background. Steven Curtis Chapman's "I Will Be Here" became a marriage promise between my husband and me. The hymn "It Is Well with My Soul" soothed my broken heart when I lost my father at 25 years of age. Whatever the occasion, there has always been a song to embrace me, to point me back to Jesus and toward his infinite love for me.

The stories in this book have greatly moved me and have reminded me of the powerful impact Christian music can have. I pray that you will find comfort within the pages of *Changed*. Moreover, I pray you will be drawn closer to God as he changes your life through the power of Christian music.

CHRISTY BARRITT

Christy Barritt is the author of *The Trouble with Perfect* and *The Waiting,* both mysteries with a touch of suspense and romance. Her articles have appeared in publications such as *Campus Life, Guideposts for Teens, Brio, Marriage Partnership,* and *The Lookout.* A Chesapeake, Virginia, native, Christy is also a weekly columnist for the *Virginian-Pilot* newspaper, and her website, www.WillWrite4Food.com, was named by *Writer's Digest* magazine in 2003 as one of the "101 Best Web Sites for Writers." Christy is the worship leader at Celebration Christian Church in Suffolk, Virginia.

GINNY'S STORY

my friends tell me that I am the only person they know who can attend a Southern Gospel concert and, at the same time, read *HM* magazine. They laugh at the fact that I will drive over a hundred miles to attend a Christian rock concert. Sometimes, I think my love for music runs as deeply as God's love
runs for me. Music is my driving force. My love for music is powerful.

Love is one of the most dynamic emotions we can ever experience. My love for music is probably the single most important reason why I am the person I am today. I cannot even begin to describe the influence Christian music has had on my life for over twenty-five years. Music started out as a hobby for me. In my early years, I would ask my dad to go with me to a Petra concert at the Ohio State Fair. Today, my mom and I are taking many exciting trips. Flying to Los Angeles to the Grammy Awards will always be a fond memory for me. My friend Karen and I oftentimes find ourselves driving to Nashville for Gospel Music Week or for the Dove Awards. It has been a fun and crazy ride.

While writing this book and reading the stories shared by the contributors, I pondered my own spiritual journey. My love for music has played a tremendous part in developing and growing my faith. God demonstrates his love for me and has inspired me to write about Christian music.

I am blessed to have the opportunity to write CD reviews, concert previews, and artist profiles for various publications. I have had the opportunity to interview many Christian artists. I could write an entire book about what I have experienced over the past ten to twelve years in the music business. I am fortunate that I have had the chance to work with most of the people involved in the contemporary Christian music industry.

I am blown away when I realize the things that God has allowed me to do with what I love so dearly. He has truly given me the desires of my heart. Music and writing have always been my two biggest passions. It amazes me to see how God brought it all together. I enjoy watching God reveal his plan for my life. I have found his purpose in unexpected ways and oftentimes through hardships. God has put me in places I never thought or imagined that I would ever be.

I had the opportunity to go on tour with Audio Adrenaline. At that point in my career, I was excited to work on a project with them.

At the same time, behind the scenes at home my dad was dying of cancer. While experiencing the opportunity of a lifetime, working on my first book, it was also a bad time to for me to go on the road. It was a very difficult decision to make.

After talking it over with my parents, however, I decided to take the trip. My dad passed away the last day of my journey with Audio A. In spite of the circumstances I was facing at the time, I stepped out in faith and lived in love. God honored my decision. He allowed his glory to be revealed in my life through that difficult situation.

God's love is tremendous and has a way of changing our lives. We can sometimes find ourselves in unusual, strange, or even broken places when God chooses to use us for his purposes. Only God's love can do something like that. This thought reminds me of one timeless song that expresses the kind of love I know.

I remember sitting in the pew of my church at the age of 12, singing "Love Lifted Me" with all my might. It is that same inspiration, expressed through all styles of music, that has been a compelling force in my life.

I see myself as a motivator and an encourager. I am able to express God's love freely to others because of the love of my family and close friends and because of God's love for me. When people see me, or consider my life's contribution, it is my desire that they will see a person who is motivated by love—the same kind of love that Jesus has for you and me.

I was sinking deep in sin,
far from a peaceful shore,
Very deeply stained within,
sinking to rise no more;
But the Master of the sea,
heard my despairing cry,
From the waters lifted me,
now safe am I.
Love lifted me! Love lifted me!
When nothing else could help,
Love lifted me.

All my heart to him I give,
ever to him I'll cling,
In his blessed presence live,
ever his praises sing;
Love so mighty and so true,
merits my soul's best songs;
Faithful loving service, too,
to him belongs.
Love lifted me! Love lifted me!
When nothing else could help,
Love lifted me.

Souls in danger, look above,
Jesus completely saves;
He will lift you by his love,
out of angry waves,
He's the Master of the sea,
billows his will obey;
He your Saviour wants to be,
be saved today.
Love lifted me! Love lifted me!
When nothing else could help,
Love lifted me.

GINNY MCCABE

Ginny is a Cincinnati native. She is an entertainment and feature writer for newspapers, magazines, and websites including *American Songwriter, Bassics, CBA Marketplace, Christian Retailing, CCM Magazine, HM Magazine, NRB Magazine, Relevant Magazine,* BGEA, Lifeway.com, and Crosswalk.com. Ginny is the author of *Some Kind of Journey: On the Road with Audio Adrenaline* and coauthor with Mary Lee Tracy on *Living the Gold-Medal Life: Inspirations from Female Athletes.* She also contributed to *Rock Stars on God: 20 Artists Speak Their Minds About Faith* by Doug Van Pelt.

DEEP ENOUGH TO DREAM

// PERFORMED BY CHRIS RICE //

Lazy summer afternoon
Screened in porch and nothin' to do
I just kicked off my tennis shoes
Slouchin' in a plastic chair
Rakin' my fingers through my hair
I close my eyes and I leave them
    there
And I yawn, and sigh, and slowly
    fade away

Chorus:
Deep enough to dream in brilliant
    colors
I have never seen
Deep enough to join a billion people
For a wedding feast
Deep enough to reach out and touch
The face of the One who made me
And oh, the love I feel, and oh the
    peace
Do I ever have to wake up

Awakened by a familiar sound
A clumsy fly is buzzin' around
He bumps the screen and he tumbles
    down
He gathers about his wits and pride
And tries again for the hundredth
    time
'Cause freedom calls from the other
    side
And I smile and nod, and slowly drift
    away

Chorus

'Cause peace is pouring over my soul
See the lambs and the lions playin'
I join in and I drink the music
Holiness is the air I'm breathin'
My faithful heroes break the bread
And answer all of my questions
Not to mention what the streets are
    made of
My heart's held hostage by this love

And these brilliant colors I have never
    seen
I join a billion people for a wedding feast
And I reach out and touch the face of
    the One who made me
Deep enough to dream in brilliant colors
    I have never seen
Deep enough to join a billion people for
    a wedding feast
Deep enough to reach out and touch the
    face of the One who made me
And oh, the love I feel, and oh the peace
Do I ever have to wake up
Do I ever have to wake up
Do I really have to wake up now

/// DECIDING TO FORGIVE ///

BY BEVERLY HOLLIDAY

as I walked through the office, the whispers of my coworkers caused tension to settle across my neck. I had been hearing the mumbled conversations for weeks. It wasn't unusual for the hushed tones to stop as soon as I was near. Finally, I approached a coworker about it.

She told me that my husband, who worked for the same company, was having an affair with one of my coworkers. It seemed everyone knew about the affair except me. My colleague was eager to supply me with the juicy details of everything that had gone on. I barely heard her.

The word "affair" continuously echoed throughout my mind. Could it be true?

I knew something was wrong in my marriage. My husband wasn't coming straight home at night after work. It was usually a few hours later. He had become easily angered. It seemed the kids and I had to walk on eggshells around him. On his days off, he oftentimes disappeared for hours with only a flimsy explanation. I was suspicious from the beginning. My husband and I were drifting apart, but it seemed there was nothing I could do about it.

A part of me couldn't believe my husband was having an affair. Shame and betrayal choked me. How could he do this to me or to the children? We had once been so happy together. How could things have gone so wrong?

I knew I had to talk to my husband. I asked him if the rumors were true. Initially, he denied the affair. He insisted that he and the other woman were just friends. But my coworkers continually set me straight. He was cheating on me and blatantly lying about it. After some persistence, he finally admitted that he was having an affair, but he also insisted our coworker was the one who chased him. I threatened divorce. My husband vowed to end the affair. He begged me to give him another chance.

In the beginning, I was consumed with anger. I just wanted to go to a far away place. I couldn't believe our lives had turned into a soap opera. How could this have happened? We were involved in a church, went to Sunday school, and had Christian friends.

In the midst of our marriage crisis, I realized I needed to turn it over to God. It sounds simple, but it wasn't. I couldn't change my husband or control anything that was happening in my life. I began listening to Christian talk radio and Christian music stations.

I continued to listen to secular music, as well. I heard many songs about lost love, betrayal, or winning someone back. I couldn't stand hearing anything that reminded me of what I was going through. As a result, I started listening exclusively to Christian music stations. There, I heard songs about the love of Jesus. The music helped me focus on him and not on my problems.

Eventually, I bought a CD which featured various Christian artists. The song "Deep Enough to Dream" by Chris Rice was on the CD. I immediately warmed to his voice. In addition, I admired the way he told a story with his lyrics.

The song was about going to heaven and sharing the wedding feast with Christ. It reminded me that I needed to focus on heavenly things, instead of worrying about the problems I was facing on earth. The entire song spoke to me, but I especially liked the lines:

> Deep enough to join a billion people
> For the wedding feast.
> Deep enough to reach out and touch
> The face of the One who made me
> All the love I feel and all the peace
> Do I ever have to wake up?

I wanted to stay in that place! A line at the end of the song said, "My heart's held hostage by this love." I really needed the love of Christ during that time. The song reminded me of my priorities. I immediately knew what I had to do.

I loved my husband and our children. I knew I had to forgive him and the woman with whom he was involved, even if he didn't change. Things didn't happen overnight, but once I made the decision to forgive, a huge burden was lifted. I persevered with God's help.

I filled my life with Christian music. Songs by Rich Mullins, Michael W. Smith, Steven Curtis Chapman, Gary Chapman, and many others helped change my outlook on life. I was committed to Christ. I knew I could get through anything if I kept my focus on him. Christian music helped me block out the problems of the world.

After seven months, my husband came to his senses, through the power of prayer. He later told me he was influenced by the evidence of Christ in my life and the Christian music that constantly played in our home. After rededicating his life to Christ and making a complete change, he couldn't listen to secular music either!

We have now been married eighteen years. Filling my life with Christian music helped me cope with crisis, grow in my faith, and forgive those who had hurt me.

BEVERLY HOLIDAY

Beverly lives in Tennessee with her husband and two teenage children. She is active in her local church.

THE ANCHOR HOLDS

// PERFORMED BY RAY BOLTZ //

I have journeyed
Through the long, dark night
Out on the open sea
By faith alone
Sight unknown
And yet his eyes were watching me.

Chorus:
The anchor holds
Though the ship is battered
The anchor holds
Though the sails are torn
I have fallen on my knees
As I faced the raging seas
But the anchor holds
In spite of the storm.

I've had visions
And I've had dreams
I've even held them in my hand
But I never knew
They could slip right through
Like they were only
Grains of sand.

Chorus

Now I have been young
And I'm older now
And there has been beauty
These eyes have seen
But it was in the night
In the storms of my life
That's when God proved
His love to me.

Chorus

TOSSED BUT NOT DEFEATED

BY CANDACE POPE

/// ///

ife was spinning out of control. My fifteen-year-old son, Ben, had been complaining of a headache for more than a week. Thinking it was probably a sinus infection, I took him to the doctor.

"Leukemia?" I questioned as the doctor gave us the grim diagnosis.

Several hours later, after a long drive to a large children's hospital, I stood at Ben's bedside. The doctor explained that the three years of chemotherapy wouldn't be so bad. He told us that Ben's main problem would be fatigue. He also felt that Ben would be able to return to high school and graduate on time. Like any teenager Ben was more concerned about his appearance than his health. Ben was encouraged when the doctor said he wouldn't lose weight. "Well, at least I won't look like a cancer victim," he said through clenched teeth.

We didn't realize the nightmare had just begun. The doctor explained that Ben would have to be in the hospital initially for five days. That was two days longer than usual because he was admitted on a weekend. But we didn't leave the hospital until eleven days later.

After two days of constant blood transfusions and intravenous fluids, Ben developed severe pneumonia. This delayed the surgery needed for inserting the special IV tube into his chest. Coughing was torture because of Ben's severe headache and a temporary IV that was inserted into his neck. Radiation treatments to the head were delayed, not only because of the extended hospital stay, but also because Ben developed shingles on his head.

Ben was kept in isolation for two weeks. He hadn't lost his hair, so the pain of the shingles was intensified whenever the doctors or nurses tried to check the lesions on his scalp.

By the time the doctors started the radiation treatments, Ben had developed a severe, debilitating headache caused by numerous spinal taps done to check for leukemia cells in the spinal fluid. The radiation intensified the headache. The pain medication caused more vomiting. Climbing in and out of the car in 95 degree weather every day to go to the treatment facility didn't help, either. I parked the car directly in front of the door, would leave the air conditioning on, and run to get a wheelchair.

By the time Ben's thick brown hair had disappeared, he had also lost twenty-five pounds. Bald, skinny, and all but lost in the whiteness of the hospital sheets, Ben was so weak he could hardly walk without assistance.

But soon we were home again. After many weeks of special IV fluid, which I connected to the tube in his chest at night, Ben had gained back some of the weight and was feeling stronger.

During the remaining years of treatment, Ben had several severe reactions to medications, and permanent damage to the cartilage in his knees and elbows caused by the chemotherapy. The spinal headache, weakness, and low blood counts prevented him from attending classes, but a tutor came to the house on the days when Ben was well enough.

The "good" days were few and far between, unfortunately. I remember one particularly bad day. I grabbed the phone on the fourth ring. Pastor Marv was calling to ask how I was doing.

"Ben's blood work was good yesterday, so he took the chemo," I said. "He has been throwing up all morning."

"You have been on my mind this morning, so I just thought I should call. You sound awfully tired." It didn't occur to me that Marv had asked about me rather than Ben.

"So, God told you to call me, huh?" I said with a weak laugh. "That's interesting, especially since I have been wondering where he is in all this misery. I can't seem to get in touch with him any more."

I explained how I was depending heavily on the prayers of the church, since I was consumed with getting Ben well again. All I could say to God was, "Help! Help!"

Lovingly, Marv reminded me that there were many people continuously praying for our family. He admitted he didn't understand a lot of things, but there was one thing he knew for sure: God is God.

"Candace, have you heard the song 'The Anchor Holds'? Well, what the song says is true. God is right where he was yesterday and right where he will be tomorrow. I know you must feel like a battered sailboat, lost at sea, but God knows exactly where you are, and he has a firm hold on you. He is still in control."

His words were exactly what I needed to hear. How reassuring to be reminded that things weren't really spinning out of control. I could still depend on God to hold me tightly when I was totally unsteady.

Before Ben's illness, I had grown complacent. I had placed God on a shelf and had skipped along my own merry and busy way. I thought I had things under control. My ship seemed to be sailing along fairly well, so who needed an anchor, anyway?

But when the storm hit, I became acutely aware of my need for an anchor. Suddenly, I was bouncing and spinning. I needed to know when the storm was over, I would be right where I was supposed to be, attached to the anchor of my soul.

Years after that long dark night, I am able to see how God proved his love to me, as the song says. He proved it through the faithfulness of the wonderful people in both my own church and in many others, as they prayed without ceasing. God proved his love for me by allowing me to come back to him after I had pulled away. And he proved his love with a phone call from my pastor, to remind me that the anchor holds, in spite of the storm.

CANDACE POPE

Candace lives in Southeastern Ohio with her husband, where they own and manage a small business. They have three grown children. Ben completed his chemotherapy in 1998. He is now a sixth-grade teacher in Georgia.

ALLELUJAH

// UNKNOWN //

Allelujah. Allelujah. Allelujah. Allelujah.
Allelujah. Allelujah. Allelujah. Allelujah.

Unknown. Public domain.

ONE MOMENT TO REMEMBER

/// ///

BY CAROLYN R. BENNETT

the woman in the hospital bed was not the woman I remembered. Wrinkles and dark blotches covered her skin. Her hair had been pulled away from her face into a matted and tangled knot behind her head. Although she was covered with a threadbare nightgown, I noticed that she had lost even more weight. The woman in the hospital bed was not my grandmother. Time, dementia, and old age had stolen my grandmother from me.

I stared at the shell of the person in front of me. I was trying to catch of a glimpse of the woman I once knew. I looked for the smile that once welcomed me at her front door. I wanted to smell the aroma of hamburgers cooking on the grill. But most of all, I longed to crawl up in her lap and hear her tell me again that God was in control and that everything would be okay.

Instead, she was still. Her face was expressionless. The room was silent except for the pulsating beat of the heart monitor behind her bed. Her skin was rough and beaten with age. The room reeked of ammonia and Lysol. Tears began to swell in my eyes. Behind her closed eyes, the woman of faith I remembered, no longer existed.

Three years earlier, I first noticed her change. She insisted that children had invaded her house and were stealing her money. She accused my grandfather of having an affair. One Saturday afternoon I called to check on her. She thought I was my mother. She talked to two children in the room, whom she thought was my sister and me. The diagnosis was grim. Dementia had taken control of her mind.

Meanwhile, schleraderma had ravaged her body. Several organs including her lungs and liver had severe scarring. We all knew that the disease would eventually kill her. The only question was when.

I visited my grandmother several times at Northeast Medical. She had fallen, and my grandfather had rushed her to the emergency room. Fluid filled her lungs, and the doctors recommended that she remain in ICU until the infection cleared up. Most of the time, she remained unconscious. Occasionally, she stirred, briefly catching her breath, and shifting her position. A few times, she opened her eyes. She stared vacantly at the ceiling acknowledging no one.

I felt hopeless. She didn't even know I was in the room with her. Most days, I simply kept my grandfather company. He visited her every day, arriving after breakfast and leaving just before dinner. He welcomed the opportunity to talk to her.

But this particular day, grandfather was late. He had gone to the grocery story to pick up a few items. Some of the nurses scurried down the hallway of the ICU wing. A few stood chatting by the nurse's station. I sat alone in my grandmother's room watching her sleep.

Suddenly, I heard a stir from the bed. I looked up from the book I was reading. Grandmother had not moved. Her eyes remained closed. She took a couple deep breaths and in a raspy alto voice began to sing: "Allelujah. Allelujah. Allelujah. Allelujah."

I stood up and quickly walked over to her bedside. The railing was cold, but warmth radiated from the bed. I cleared my throat and joined her with a soprano harmony: "Allelujah. Allelujah. Allelujah. Allelujah."

For a brief moment, grandmother paused and listened as I sang. The nurses outside continued to rush around, taking care of the other patients. All the noise seemed to fade away into the background. Even the incessant beeping of the heart monitor blended into the background unheard.

After a moment, my grandmother's voice, barely above a whisper, joined in with mine: "Allelujah. Allelujah. Allelujah. Allelujah." As she sang, she lifted her shaky left hand into the air. Her fingers opened in worship to God. Yes, somewhere deep inside, my grandmother still lived.

She continued to sing for the next couple of minutes before her voice faded away. I stood by her bedside watching her fade back into unconsciousness. The warmth in her face disappeared. Her hand dropped back to her side. Although her breathing remained steady, all life within her was gone.

My grandmother lived for another three months. Most of the time, she slept. During the brief moments when she was conscious, she was delusional. At times, she knitted imaginary threads together as she sat in bed. Some days, she yelled at my mom or me for not allowing her to return home, where she thought she belonged.

She died quickly during another visit to the hospital. My grandfather had just left her side and was on his way home for dinner when she left this world.

For months, I told no one about that day in the hospital. It had been a cherished gift and one last precious memory of who my grandmother was and how she had impacted my life. I will carry that memory with me forever.

CAROLYN R. BENNETT

Carolyn is the Editor and Publications Coordinator for Accelerating International Mission Strategies (AIMS) where she has had the opportunity to travel around the world as a missionary journalist and photographer. In her hometown of Virginia Beach, she teaches English at a local community college and ministers in music at her local church.

TAKE MY HAND AND WALK

// **PERFORMED BY THE KRY** //

I know there are times your dreams turn
to dust.
You wonder as you cry
Why it has to hurt so much.
Give me all your sadness
Someday you will know the reason why,
With a childlike heart,
simply put your trust in me.

Chorus:
Take my hand and walk where I lead,
Keep your eyes on me alone.
Don't you say why were the old days
better,
Just because you're scared of the
unknown,
Take my hand and walk.

Don't live in the past,
Cuz yesterday's gone,
Wishin' memories would last,
You're afraid to carry on.
But you don't know what's comin',
but you know the one who holds
tomorrow.
I will be your guide,
Take you through the night,
If you keep your eyes on Me.

Take my hand and walk where I lead.
Keep your eyes on me alone,
Don't you say why were the old days
better,
Just because you're scared of the
unknown.
Take my hand and walk where I lead.
You will never be alone.
Faith is to be sure of what you hope for,
And the evidence of things unseen,
So take my hand and walk.

Bridge
Just like a child holding daddy's hand,
Don't let go of mine,
You know you can't stand on your own.

Repeat chorus

/// GOD WILL HOLD MY HAND ///

BY DANIELLE HELLER

The rain pounded down upon the car as my friend and I drove down the rural Kentucky road. The windshield wipers were running at full speed. I wondered as we drove along what my life would hold. Similar to the blurry road before us, the future seemed hazy.

In a month, I would graduate from college. Many important decisions hung over my head. Would I stay in the area or move back home? Would I pursue a career in music or would I take a more reasonable, stable job? Should I settle down at all? Or should I use this time to travel and explore the world? My future seemed uncertain. I longed for my college days to never end. How I wished the road before me would be clear.

My friend pulled onto a grocery store parking lot. I waited for her in the car, while she went inside. "You have to hear this song," she said. She slipped a cassette tape into the player, darted from the car, and then disappeared into the rain. A moment later, lyrics hummed from the speakers.

> Take my hand and walk where I lead.
> Keep your eyes on me alone.
> Don't you say why were the old days better,
> Just because you're scared of the unknown.

Tears welled in my eyes. I realized the words reflected my innermost feelings. Because of my fear of the future, I was holding on to the past. This new stage of my life had tossed me out of my comfort zone. All I had known my entire life was school. Now for the first time, I was facing the real world.

I listened closely to the next verse. "Don't live in the past, cause yesterday's come. Wishing memories would last. You're afraid to carry on. But you don't know what's coming. But you know the one who holds tomorrow. I will be your guide, take you through the night, if you keep your eyes on me."

Each line spoke directly to the place I was in life. A messenger from above could have sung the song. The song reminded me that God was in control of my future and as long as I held tightly to him, I would be okay. Though the decisions seemed overwhelming, I knew God held my dreams. With him leading, there was no need to look back and mourn over days passed.

> The bridge of the song was the final balm to my heart.
> Just like a child holding daddy's hand,
> Don't let go of Mine,
> You know you can't stand on your own.

I thought back to the days of my youth and how I knew everything would be okay as long as Daddy was by my side. He would protect me, provide for me, and nurture me. I knew I never had to worry while my earthly father protected me. I realized that taking this next step in life would be okay. It was simply a time to hold my heavenly Father's hand.

As I approach trials in my life, I oftentimes look back at this song. It reminds me to look toward the future and to trust in God. It is too easy to focus on the past and mourn over days gone. But if we hold on to God's hand, we can be assured that he is in full control. He won't let us fall.

DANIELLE HELLER

Danielle is a music minister who lives on the East Coast. She enjoys playing the guitar, singing, and ministering to those who are hurting.

EASTER SONG

// **PERFORMED BY KEITH GREEN** //

Hear the bells ringing,
They're singing that you can be born
   again,
Here the bells ringing,
They're singing Christ is risen from the
   dead.
The angel up on the tombstone,
Said he has risen, just as he said,
Quickly now, go tell his disciples,
That Jesus Christ is no longer dead.

Joy to the word, he has risen, hallelujah,
He's risen, hallelujah,
He's risen, hallelujah.

Hear the bells ringing,
They're singing that you can be healed
   right now,
Hear the bells ringing, they're singing,
Christ, he will reveal it now,
The angels, they all surround us,
And they are ministering Jesus' power,
Quickly now, reach out and receive it,
For this could be your glorious hour.

Joy to the world, he has risen, hallelujah,
He's risen, hallelujah,
He's risen, hallelujah, hallelujah.

The angel up on the tombstone,
Said he has risen, just as he said,
Quickly now, go tell his disciples,
That Jesus Christ is no longer dead.

Joy to the world, he has risen, hallelujah,
He's risen, hallelujah,
He's risen, hallelujah, hallelujah.

/// CHANGED BY THE BELLS ///

BY CLARE CARTAGENA

I pulled the covers over my cold nose. I was trying to hang on to the last shred of the night. I convinced myself it couldn't possibly be time to get up. As I buried deeper into the blankets, I fought impending consciousness by imagining a snowstorm had closed school for the day.

Every kid in town dreamed of the same thing at least once during the winter months. I decided to drift back into this fantasy, almost falling back to sleep again. Then I was awakened by a sound from the kitchen. It traveled down the short hallway of our apartment in waves.

"Hear those bells ringing. They're ringing you can be born again," a cheery choir sang. I jumped out of my bed in a whirlwind of confusion. What was this noise? In my short thirteen years of life, I had never heard anything like it before.

I rushed into the kitchen. The radio was playing full-blast. "Hear those bells ringing. They're ringing Christ is risen from the dead."

There my father stood. He was wearing an apron and holding a bowl with pancake batter dripping down the sides and onto his hands. Was I dreaming? For a few seconds, I wondered which was worse—a domestic dad cooking breakfast or the exuberant choir ruining my sleep.

"Good morning," my father said grinning from ear to ear. I was so surprised that I could not respond back. What could a thirteen year old say when her strict, authoritative dad suddenly seemed to have melted down with religion?

"Was this the man I had called Dad for all these years?" I asked myself. I certainly did not understand this new music he was playing, nor did I want any part of it. I crept back to my room, resigned to begin another day.

Later that day, my father told me that he had been born again. I bounced that thought around in my head for awhile. I then came to the same conclusion all my friends did when such things were mentioned. My father was crazy.

I didn't understand all this talk about God and Jesus. Sure, I knew some things about God. Church attendance was a weekly event around our house. We faithfully recited the blessing each night before we ate dinner. Christmas and Easter reminded me about God each year. I didn't need to be like my father, however. He began telling people that Jesus loved them. I did not need to play lame songs from the radio. My father had surely changed when he became born again, but I did not like it. As a matter of fact I didn't want any part of it.

Morning after morning, at exactly six thirty, the same song rang out throughout our house, regardless of how I felt about it. The words were happy and filled with hope.

"Hear those bells ringing. They're ringing you can be born again."

"I don't want to be born again," I cried, one morning as I listened to the song playing from the kitchen. "I don't want to become like a greeting card. That kind of life is not for me." I was having enough trouble with being what I thought was normal without purposely being abnormal. I groaned and sought out a few more minutes in bed with pillows sandwiched over my head. I wondered how I would survive such abuse.

By the end of the first week, however, I found myself singing the song in the shower. I quickly turned it into a mocking rendition, exaggerating the sweetness. Was the plan to wear me down until I gave up?

"Yeah, yeah, I hear the bells," I said to the radio the following morning. "They are definitely ringing in my head."

Did my dad have to keep the volume turned up so loudly that I was jolted awake every day? I sat at the table eating my crepes, with peach syrup, wondering just how long my father could keep this niceness up. Maybe he would wear down and the music would go away with his enthusiasm.

"Would you like to go to a church meeting tonight?" Dad asked me breaking the silence.

"Go to church when it is not Sunday?" I questioned. "Why?"

"It's fun," he answered. "We sing songs, read from the Bible and pray. You could learn more about God," he added.

The idea struck a chord. There was a desire buried within me to find something deeper and more real about God. I wanted something more touchable than tradition and just following rules.

My father waited quietly, not taking a breath while I considered my answer. "Okay," I said. I didn't want to let my father down. "I will go at least one time."

That evening, as I followed my father into the meeting, I dragged my feet. "I hope this doesn't go on too late," I said. "I have homework to do. Maybe another night would be better." My father smiled at me, but he never stopped walking.

Inside, rows of folding chairs cramped the church basement. A pianist played off-key scales. To her left, the one and only cool looking guy in the building stood up with a guitar. My spirits perked up somewhat when I saw him. "Maybe this was not going to be so bad," I thought. About the time I settled into that thought, a girl joined him. She squeezed his hand and then began to lead the singing with a high-pitched melodious voice. I expected at any moment she would sing, "Hear those bells ringing. They're ringing you can be born again."

The meeting closed with an upbeat song about banners held high. Everyone stood up and waved their arms. It looked like an exercise class for senior citizens. I refused to join them. During that meeting, I was subjected to gushing smiles of approval from my father's friends— all older women. I did a good job looking sweet. They had no idea how much I wanted to get out of there, however.

"No. This is not the life I want," I repeated to myself.

The next morning, with no mercy, the relentless bells rang again. "I don't want to be born again," I screamed inside.

God didn't respond to my foolish claims, however. Again and again,

He brought the flame of his word to my life as the radio played. I heard both music and spiritual messages anytime I entered the kitchen.

Though I did not want to admit it, these new ideas were taking root. New thoughts replaced the old. Somehow, a fire was ignited in my heart for God. Suddenly, Jesus was in the forefront of my mind.

Baby step by baby step, God led me ever closer to the place where I not only knew I needed a Savior but I wanted him to be my Savior. If that meant I became a Jesus freak, spouting scriptures and talking about God's love, then so be it. I found that when I fully accepted Jesus, God by his wonderful grace, accepted me just the way I was. I was still shy and unsure of myself, but I was also hungry for more of him.

Years later, I heard the song once again. The voice that sang loudly, clearly, and beautifully full of faith came from my own lips.

"Hear those bells ringing. They're ringing you can be born again."

I suddenly remembered the first morning that those bells rang into my dark, love-silent life. As I sang, my heart swelled with joy and gratitude for my transformation. I thanked God for taking me from the place where I mocked the words of that song to the place where tears of joy blessed me. I heard the bells ringing. And I was born again.

CLARE CARTAGENA

Clare lives in Northwest New Jersey with her husband and two teenage children. Clare's desire is to use her published stories, devotionals, and book reviews to "fan into flame the gift of God" in others. She is a member of the North Jersey Christian Writers Group and teaches Sunday school at her church.

WHAT A FRIEND

// PERFORMED BY JOSEPH M. SCRIVEN //

What a Friend we have in Jesus
All our sins and griefs to bear!
What a privilege to carry
Everything to God in prayer!
O what peace we often forfeit
O what needless pain we bear
All because we do not carry
Everything to God in prayer

Have we trials and temptations?
Is there trouble anywhere?
We should never be discouraged;
Take it to the Lord in prayer.
Can we find a friend so faithful
Who will all our sorrows share?
Jesus knows our every weakness;
Take it to the Lord in prayer.

Are we weak and heavy laden,
Cumbered with a load of care?
Precious Savior, still our refuge,
Take it to the Lord in prayer.
Do your friends despise, forsake you?
Take it to the Lord in prayer!
In his arms He'll take and shield you;
You will find a solace there.

Blessed Savior, Thou hast promised
Thou wilt all our burdens bear
May we ever, Lord, be bringing
All to Thee in earnest prayer.
Soon in glory bright unclouded
There will be no need for prayer
Rapture, praise and endless worship
Will be our sweet portion there.

/// A FRIEND IN JESUS ///

BY DEBORAH WHITE

I sat beside my mother's bedside studying her weary expression. Even though, I knew she would be better off to leave this world behind, I also knew how much I would miss her. In addition, my children would miss not having their grandmother to celebrate the days ahead.

For a little over three years, Mom had battled breast cancer. My family knew her time with us on earth was coming to an end. Her mother and sisters traveled from Ohio to Virginia to help care for her. Mother's final days were spent not only with the best care at home, but with loving care. They shared memories with her, cried with her, encouraged her, and visited with the many people she had befriended over the years.

It was hard to believe that Mom's journey was coming to an end. I realized that I was losing not only my mother, but also my best friend. Over the years, she had been my mentor, my companion, my counselor, and my confidante. Mom taught me about God and his love for me.

From the time I was just a tot, my mother had taken my brothers and me to church. I was baptized at the age of twelve. It was seven years later, however when I understood my need for a Savior and accepted Jesus as my Lord. Mom soon followed. We were baptized together.

A sense of heaviness pressed on my chest, as I mourned days lost. Mother had become too weak and disoriented to speak. She oftentimes journeyed between her childhood and adult years. She hallucinated and became confused as time went on.

As I held her hand and watched my mother near the end of her journey, I felt tears spring to my eyes. For my own selfish reasons, I wanted Mom to stay. I cherished the comforting feeling of having my mother by my side.

Thoughts of her dying began to overwhelm me, while grief welled up inside my heart. I buried my head into the bed, trying to make sense of everything I felt. Then to my surprise, I heard humming.

I raised my head. I was trying to figure out where the music was coming from. I glanced at my mother's face. Her eyes were closed and she was in a great deal of pain. Regardless, she was humming a tune.

I recognized the song as "What a Friend We Have in Jesus." I wasn't sure my mother knew I was there, but she was definitely aware of Jesus' presence. Mom had traveled paths where none of us could go, but Jesus could and had.

Mom passed on a message of comfort through that song. We had sung "What a Friend We Have in Jesus" oftentimes at church. I knew most of the words, but realized that I had never felt the words deeply within my heart.

My priorities had been out of focus. I was busy in my church, but I wasn't the servant I should have been. I wasn't always kind or patient. I knew God was in control of all things, but I didn't trust him to handle things in my life. I didn't take my hurts and despair to him.

The song reminded me that I could give all the pain, the sadness, the restlessness, and fear I was feeling to Jesus. Even in Mom's confusion and discomfort she was sure of Jesus' friendship to her and his faithfulness to give her peace.

It has been twenty years since my mother went to be with her Friend, Jesus. Whenever I think of her, however, I remember the hope I found through the words of this song.

We have been told throughout the scriptures that on earth we will face trials and temptations. This song reminds us, however, that we have a Friend who will bear our sins and our grief. Too often, I have carried needless pain and burdens because I forgot that God willingly gave me that privilege.

Sometimes, I find myself humming this tune to myself. It reminds me to carry everything to God. In the midst of pain, the words have comforted me. In the midst of confusion, the song has been my light. In grief, the melody has given me peace. "What a Friend We Have in Jesus" reminds me of God's promises to his children.

DEBBIE WHITE

Debbie has been married thirty-one years and has four children and three grandchildren. She works as a teacher assistant and enjoys reading and creative writing.

FRIEND OF A WOUNDED HEART

// PERFORMED BY THE BROOKLYN TABERNACLE CHOIR //

Smile—Make 'em think you're happy
Lie—And say that things are fine
And hide that empty longing that you feel
Don't ever show it
Just keep your heart concealed

Why—Are the days so lonely
Where can a heart go free
And who will dry the tears that no one's seen
There must be someone
To share your silent dreams

Chorus

Caught like a leaf in the wind
Lookin' for a friend—Where can you turn
Whisper the words of a prayer—And you'll find him there
Arms open wide—Love in his eyes

Jesus—He meets you where you are
Jesus—He heals you secret scars
All the love you're longing for is
Jesus—The friend of a wounded heart

RUNNING AWAY
/// FROM IT ALL ///

BY IDALIA ROSA-MARTINEZ

I swung my waist-length dark hair in pendulum sways, keeping step with the rhythm of Janice Joplin as she wailed, "Feels like a ball and chain." I understood her song. Adolescent rules felt like a ball and chain to me, "dragging me down."

From my early teens, song lyrics grabbed me and dictated the story of my life. I was caught up in the "flower child/sexual revolution era." Nothing—not even threats from my parents—was going to cut me loose from my music. Music helped me escape my adolescent insecurities and a disintegrating home life, as I searched for the meaning of life.

I first ran away from home when I was thirteen. "Runaway Child, Running Wild" by The Temptations, echoed in my mind. I couldn't stand watching my mother being battered, nor my father's drinking.

My first departure from home didn't last long. My runaway attempts continued, however. With each attempt, I stayed gone approximately one month. But I matured with each try. Life's experiences have a way of causing a person to grow up quickly.

My parents later divorced. A song by the Temptations became my theme, "Papa Was a Rolling Stone." Disgust replaced the love I once had for my father. That disgust grew greater each time I heard the words from the song, "Wherever he laid his hat was his home." I felt the pain of a father's abandoned love. I questioned my worthiness since I didn't have a normal family. We had become a spectacle of the neighborhood as midnight visits from the police became frequent events.

I always felt inadequate. My pain and worthlessness grew stronger as the words from the Diana Ross and The Supremes' "Love Child" rang in my ears. The lyrics talked about a girl never being "quite as good."

That song spoke volumes to the pain and circumstances of my life.

My siblings nursed their growing pains in their own ways. I nursed mine by becoming a single mother at the age of seventeen. I decided to go out into the world alone. The journey was long and empty. I was forged by the power of many song lyrics that justified my action of the times, such as "Love the One You're With."

My life felt empty. The pain I felt as a child haunted me. Peace seemed a distant reality as I hurried through my days. I tried to ignore the void in my heart.

Several years later, a friend told me about Jesus. She invited me to go with her to prayer meetings, church services, and concerts. I considered her invitations, but always refused. She gave me a Brooklyn Tabernacle Choir album. While listening to it, I found something my heart had desperately needed to hear. The soloist sang these words:

> Jesus—He meets you where you are
> Jesus—He heals your secret scars
> All the love you're longing for is
> Jesus—The friend of a wounded heart

My heart was deeply wounded as the result of twenty years on the run, or "twenty years in the pit," as I called that period of my life. I played the song endlessly, long into the night. With my face pressed against the pillow I cried. "Could you really be my friend, God, after all I have done?" I asked.

In isolation, I continued the same ritual for weeks. Finally, my friend invited me to a live concert where the soloist of the Brooklyn Tabernacle would be performing. I attended the concert and listened as he sang:

> Smile—Make 'em think you're happy
> Lie—And say that things are fine
> And hide that empty longing that you feel
> Don't ever show it
> Just keep your heart concealed
> Why—Are the days so lonely
> Where can a heart go free

And who will dry the tears that no one's seen
There must be someone
To share your silent dreams

Tears rushed down my cheeks. I felt a sense of desperation to know more about the God who would forgive me and be my friend. I didn't know how to ask the questions I had, however. I left the concert deeply touched and grateful, but still afraid of expressing my feelings to anyone.

I listened to the familiar song each night. My grieving heart sought comfort in its words. Finally, through my desperation, I cried out to the Lord to come into my life and change it for the better. I felt a weight lifted from my heart that I had never felt before. In that moment, I felt a God I had never known. I knew I was hearing from the Almighty God who spoke back to me with love and comfort. The Brooklyn Tabernacle Choir became my first communication with Jesus.

From that day forward, I felt the strength to ask questions that were hindering me and standing in the way of true joy for my life. Through a song, God turned my life around. Suddenly, I once again found myself running. This time, however, I ran into the arms of God.

Lookin' for a friend—Where can you turn
Whisper the words of a prayer—
And you'll find him there
Arms open wide—Love in his eyes
Jesus—He meets you where you are
Jesus—He heals you secret scars
All the love you're longing for is
Jesus—The friend of a wounded heart

IDALIA ROSA-MARTINEZ

Idalia pursues a full-time writing career telling the stories of everyday people. Idalia currently resides in Chesapeake, Virginia, with her loving husband who faithfully inspires her and her characters.

YOUR LOVE

// PERFORMED BY THE PAUL COLMAN TRIO //

Your love is everything to me
Your love is everything to me
I'm so glad you found me
I'm so glad I found you
I'm so glad I listened to you whisper in my ear
You told me that you loved me
You told me I was lovely
You overlooked the ugly
And you washed away my fear
Your love is everything to me
To me

And it's all I want
It's all I have
And it's all I see
And it's all I need
It's your love.

Your love defines me
Builds and refines me
Your love is pure and real
And holy, holy

/// GOD'S HEALING LOVE ///

BY ELLIE JONES

the nightmares hit me at full-force, jarring me from sleep. I jerked up in bed and rubbed my temples. A cold sweat prickled across my otherwise warm skin. My dreams had forced me to relive horrible memories I had long tried to forget.

I tried to regain control of my breathing and force my mind away from the memories. But I couldn't. Nausea threatened to materialize. My entire body shook. The dreams seemed so real. It felt like the event was happening all over again. The dreams forced me to relive a time in life I would have rather pretended never happened.

From the time I was four, I was abused physically, emotionally, and sexually. The ugly reality ended when I was nineteen. The scars on my body and on my heart remained, however. Ten years later, when I thought the flashbacks could no longer hurt me they reared their ugly heads and made me feel like a defenseless child again.

I curled into a fetal position in my bed. I tried desperately to shake the memories. I had healed from a great deal of the abuse I suffered, but I found that I had simply pushed the worse of it to the back of my mind.

I didn't want to face the pain again. I wanted to forget it. A recent medical procedure brought memories back to the surface once again. In my pain, I cried out to Jesus.

"Please heal this problem, Jesus," I whispered. "It hurts so much."

The abuse had destroyed my perception of God. I had been taught that God loved me, but I didn't understand how. I was so confused that sometimes I had trouble loving myself—so why would God?

Over the next few weeks, I felt God answering my prayer. His love began healing me. He reminded me of who he was. I could feel him holding me, reassuring me that I was his child. I finally felt a sense of peace. I knew, however, that the process was only the beginning. I knew I needed to be quiet and listen to God's direction. I also knew healing would take time.

One day, when I was home alone, I walked past the stereo and hit play. The Paul Colman Trio's CD "One" was in the player. Familiar lyrics played through the speakers.

Even though the CD was relatively new, I particularly liked a certain song. I started to forward it to that song, but stopped. I felt the Spirit guiding me to another song—"Your Love." As the song began, the truth I needed rang out in every line.

> Your love is everything to me
> Your love is everything to me
> I'm so glad you found me
> I'm so glad I found you
> I'm so glad I listened to you
> Whisper in my ear
> You told me that you loved me
> You told me I was lovely
> You overlooked the ugly
> And you washed away my fear
>
> Your love is everything to me, to me
>
> It's all I want
> It's all I have
> And it's all I see
> And it's all I need
> And it's your love.

I realized that was exactly what Jesus had been saying and doing. He was allowing me to see myself from his perspective. At that moment, I knew his love for me couldn't be shaken by anything. I suddenly needed or wanted nothing except him. I no longer saw the trauma in my life; nor did I see myself as a broken person. The flashbacks were gone. I tangibly felt Jesus holding me and loving me.

I began singing, crying, and listening. I felt totally awash in the beauty and sheer majesty of Jesus. I was a whole person once again. My conviction grew greater with each line of the song as it continued:

> Your love defines me
> Builds and refines me
> Your love is pure and real
> And holy, holy

I sat in the kitchen, replaying the song several times. Jesus filled the room. Palatable relief and joy washed over me. All the pain and fear from my latest flashback disappeared. The joy of knowing that I was not defined by what I did, or what anyone else did to me, but only by Jesus' love was the most powerful expression I have ever experienced.

It took some time, however, to trust God enough to really allow him into some of the deeper issues in my life. For so long, I couldn't grasp the meaning of unconditional love because I never had it in my life. But slowly, God has allowed me to feel his absolute love. The security I have found in him is overwhelming.

I realized that the abuse in my past doesn't define me. Periodically, a flashback will come back to my mind. When it does, however, I ask Jesus to take it away. He answers my prayer.

God's taught me that love is always the emotion that heals. We must seek to see things from his perspective and not through our own experiences. God's love and truth has rippled throughout every aspect of my life.

"Your Love" is my worship song, my theme song, and a song of celebration all in one. I have tears of joy every time I sing it.

ELLIE JONES

Ellie is a youth worker living in Australia. Her goal is to prevent domestic violence and spare others the pain she experienced during adolescence. She works part-time in child protection and domestic violence prevention. She's passionate about showing others that they too are defined by whom they are in Jesus.

HANDS AND FEET

// **PERFORMED BY AUDIO ADRENALINE** //

An image flashed across my TV screen
Another broken heart comes in to view
I saw the pain and I turned my back
Why can't I do the things I want to?
I'm willing yet I'm so afraid
You give me strength
When I say

Chorus:
I want to be your hands
I want to be your feet
I'll go where you send me
I'll go where you send me

And I try, yeah I try
To touch the world like
You touched my life
And I find my way
To be your hands

I've abandoned every selfish thought
I've surrendered every thing I've got
You can have everything I am
And perfect everything
I'm not I'm willing,
I'm not afraid
You give me strength when I say

Chorus

This is the lifetime I turned my back
on you
From now on, I'll go so
Send me where you want me to
I finally have a mission
I promise complete
I don't need excuses
When I am your hands and feet

BEING GOD'S
/// HANDS AND FEET ///

BY JESSICA VANDER LOOP

I have always loved being a volunteer. From the time I began middle school, I knew it was important to help those who were less fortunate. The Lord gave me a servant's heart. I participated in blood drives and in Christmas parties for the handicapped. I played the piano for a senior citizens home. I was the happiest when I was volunteering. But despite the fulfillment these things brought, I still sensed something missing in my life.

During my freshman year of high school, I questioned the joy I saw in the Christians around me. Every time I saw someone who claimed to be a Christian, I wanted to know more about what triggered their happiness. I wanted to be around these people because they always seemed to be so happy. I wanted what they had.

My friend, Lauren often spoke about the fun she had at church. I wanted to experience the same joy I saw in her.

I attended a youth group with a friend. At the meeting that first night, the pastor passed out a questionnaire, which asked questions about our faith. Without fully understanding it, I completed it. Later, during the lesson, we watched a video by Audio Adrenaline. The song they sang was "Hands and Feet." The video showed people as they touched the lives of others through volunteerism.

While I watched it, I felt like God was calling me. I didn't know how to find him, however. No one had explained the gospel to me.

That night, I went home and felt convicted of my sins. I desperately wanted the Lord to come into my life. I needed to be forgiven for my transgressions.

I accepted Christ that night. I began volunteering for him. I delivered cookies to senior citizens and other people in my church. I helped my pastor at various inner city churches in D.C.

The next year, I eagerly signed up with my church for a mission trip to Quesada, Costa Rica. Other than having a personal relationship with Christ, going there was the most amazing thing that has ever happened to me. I enjoyed it so much I went again the next year!

While we were there, our group worked on a building project. We built a new home for a family of twelve. They had previously lived in a house no larger than a tool shed. I will never forget the family's first glimpse of their new living quarters, once it was complete. I knew I had made a difference in their lives. I was God's hands and feet as I worked in his mission field.

I will always remember a man, Felix. I met Felix during our first trip to Costa Rica. We painted his house. I became close to him and to his family. After I returned home, I received a letter from Felix. He wrote telling me that his heart was failing him. I was extremely concerned.

When we returned to Costa Rica the next year, the only thing I could think about was seeing Felix and finding out how he was doing. Our days were busy, however. Before I knew it our last night there had fallen upon us. I hadn't seen my friend. Felix was to be at a pastor's meeting that night, however. My friend Lauren and I went to look for him. When he wasn't there, I was heart-broken and worried.

I went back to the dining hall and cried through worship. We were singing "I Love You Lord" when a friend tapped my shoulder. She pointed toward the door.

I looked around. Felix was standing there. He looked as healthy as ever. I soon learned that the missionaries who owned the camp had prayed for Felix for a long time. Then one day, he was healed. There was absolutely nothing wrong with his heart.

Seeing Felix again was a God thing. Felix meant so much to me. I had longed to see him again and the Lord allowed it to happen.

The words of the song came back to me once again. While serving in that place, all I could think about was how I was God's hands and feet. I was doing what I was created to do; helping people and enhancing the Kingdom of God. One of the verses of "Hands and Feet" has become very important to me.

And I'll try, yeah I'll try
To touch the world like you touched my life
And I'll find my way
To be your hands
I'll abandon every selfish thought
I'll surrender every thing I've got
You can have everything I am
And perfect everything I'm not
I'm willing, I'm not afraid

Some people say it makes them feel good to volunteer simply because they feel like "they" are making a difference. It is not the same for me, however. I realize that when I help people, I'm not the one making the difference. God is working through me to make the difference. I shouldn't take any of the credit. I do it all for the glory of God.

The Lord has touched my life beyond comprehension. I want to help touch other people's lives through him. It is my desire that I will be his hands and feet wherever I go. I want to go where God sends me. I want to touch the world.

JESSICA VANDER LOOP

Jessica became a Christian during her freshman year of high school. She has a calling to become a servant of the Lord and to go wherever he sends her. It doesn't matter whether she goes, to Costa Rica, Haiti, or the streets of Baltimore. She is simply willing to go.

PRAISE THE LORD

When you're up against a struggle
That shatters all your dreams
And your hopes have been cruelly crushed
By Satan's manifested schemes
And you feel the urge within you to submit to earthly fears
Don't let the faith you're standing in seem to disappear

Chorus:
Praise the Lord
He can work through those who praise him
Praise the Lord
For our God inhabits praise
Praise the Lord
For the chains that seem to bind you
Serve only to remind you
That they drop powerless behind you
When you Praise him

Now Satan is a liar
And he wants to make us think that we are paupers
When he knows himself
We are children of the King
So lift up the mighty shield of faith for the battle must be won
We know that Jesus Christ has risen
So the work's already done!

Chorus

/// THE RACE IS STILL ON ///

BY KIM SEEVERS

"Come on Kim, you can get them!" My ears itched to hear these words. My friends' cheers baited my desire to win at any cost. "You've almost got her!"

I looked out of the corner of my eye to see my friends running along the inside track. While they cheered, my mind shifted to other things. I concentrated on passing the person in front of me. Like in every race, I replayed an ongoing story in my mind.

In a typical race, I envisioned Abraham and Sarah running ahead of me. I played a little game with myself about them being dead and beating me anyway. Sarah would laugh and clap to get me to move faster. I would also imagine many other sweet saints ahead of me, as we all made our way toward Jesus, who stood at the finish line.

Sometimes Jesus would come meet me and say, "Girl, if you want to catch me, you had better burn!"

Usually, I answered back to him, "Okay, just let me catch your robe?" That was all it took for me to win.

At the beginning of my senior year, I had already heard from two universities who were ready to offer me track scholarships. I entertained the idea of making it to the Olympics several times. Coming from a fairly poor family, I felt that I had made something of myself.

My successes were listed in the newspaper. I was making and breaking records. I won medals, ribbons, and trophies. People in my small town recognized me. They stopped to talk to me on the street, at track meets, and at the post office. I felt that all of my achievements would make me famous some day—until my senior year.

Earlier that evening, during a warm up at our district meet, I spread a large amount of deep heat sports cream on my overworked hips and hamstrings. I was running anchor for our relay team. We were really behind when the baton was passed to me. This would be my third race for the night, with one to come later.

I forced my stride to stretch as far as I could for this relay. I got into my normal imaginary state of thinking about Jesus when I passed the second place team. Suddenly, an excruciating pain ripped into my hip, causing me to falter.

"Just a cramp," I thought, "Keep going!"

The pain in my hip was too much to bear. I went down to the ground. I looked up at my coach at the end of the finish line. I wasn't thinking about anything at this time, except for the pain. My coach motioned for me to come. I got up and galloped in to win third place.

"What is it?" my coach asked.

"I don't know," I whimpered.

My friend led me to the bus, where I sat alone for the rest of the meet. In the days and weeks that followed, I went to a chiropractor who solidified my worst fear. I would be out for the rest of the season. My muscles had pulled off some bone chips. There would be no more races, medals, ribbons, or records for me. My dream of the Olympics was gone.

Oftentimes, my sister, my mother and I listened to the local Christian radio station. When our favorite songs came on, we turned the volume up and danced around, acting like we were the artists. We would sing so loudly that we would become hoarse.

One of our favorite songs was "Praise the Lord" by the Imperials. Russ Taff could sing with such passion. The song spoke about broken dreams, crushed hopes, and Satan's manifested schemes.

The song taught me that I am significant, not because of what I achieved in front of the world but because I am a child of the King. I realized that even when I faltered or failed, I was still God's child. My self worth and importance came only from and for his glory.

I am not sure what affect this song had on my sister and mother, but

I have to think that the same spirit that filled my heart with a new passion helped them, as well.

The race is still on for me. When I fall today, the King of Kings picks me up and carries me. Of course, one of my favorite verses in the Bible is about running: "Therefore, since we are surrounded by such a great cloud of witnesses, let us throw off everything that hinders and the sin that so easily entangles, and let us run with perseverance the race marked out for us" (Hebrews 12:1, NIV).

The day will come when I will cross life's finish line. I am certain that I will be holding on to his cloak.

KIM SEEVERS

Kim writes children's short stories, inspirational poems, and articles for both children and adults.

DO THEY SEE JESUS IN ME

// **PERFORMED BY JOY WILLIAMS** //

Is the face that I see in the mirror
The one I want others to see?
Do I show in the way that I walk in this
  life
The love that you've given to me?
My heart's desire is to be like you
In all that I do, all I am.

Do they see Jesus in me?
Do they recognize your face?
Do I communicate your love and your
  grace?
Do I reflect who you are
In the way I choose to be?
Do they see Jesus, Jesus in me?

Oh, it's amazing that you'd ever use me,
But use me the way you will.
Help me to hold out a heart of
  compassionate grace,
A heart that your spirit fills.
May I show forgiveness and mercy
The same way you've shown it to me.

Do they see Jesus in me?
Do they recognize your face?
Do I communicate your love and your
  grace?
Do I reflect who you are
In the way I choose to be?
Do they see Jesus, Jesus in me?

Well, I want to show all the world that
  you are
The reason they live and breathe.
So you'll be the one that they see when
  they see me.

Do they see Jesus in me?
Do they recognize your face?
Do I communicate your love and your
  grace?
Do I reflect who you are?
In the way I choose to be?
Do they see Jesus in me?
Do they see Jesus in me?

/// REFLECTING JESUS ///

BY KIM VOGEL SAWYER

Oh, no! I scrambled to retrieve the email message I had just sent, but it was too late. It was gone—irretrievable. I groaned, covering my face with my hands as my stomach churned. I wondered how I could have been so stupid!

When I drafted the email, pouring out my worry about attending the upcoming American Christian Romance Writers National Conference, I had only planned to share my thoughts with my critique group members. I felt completely comfortable with those four women. But now, thanks to a slip of the finger, I had sent the message through the entire ACRW loop of more than 500 members!

Now everyone would know that I had gained five pounds in the last three days due to my worries. Everyone would know I was stressed over leaving my family, being away from my classroom of fifth graders, and leaving my comfort zone. They would know I feared stepping into a room filled with people who knew my name but didn't really know me.

I was the ACRW List Hostess. Every week my name appeared in the email loop. Just going to conference this year had me in a state of panic. I was the "enforcer." Would my colleagues accept me or avoid me? My stomach ached constantly because of my worry. And now, everyone would be reading my secret worries and fears! How could I go to the conference and face them?

As quickly as possible, I drafted a second email, explaining my message was intended for my critique group. I asked everyone else to please ignore it. But my second message was too late. Responses were already popping into my inbox. I cringed as I opened them and began to read.

No one condemned me for my fears. In fact, people seemed to appreciate my honesty. Some confided they had similar worries. Others offered encouraging Bible verses or words of advice.

One person shared her heart with me. "When I'm facing a situation such as a conference, I make sure I go prayed up so people will see Christ in me. I pray that I can somehow be a blessing in spite of myself. Then if I really don't like what I saw in the mirror that morning, or if I feel like I said something at the table that sounded totally ditzy I can trust that God is capable of using even my inadequacies to bless someone else."

I considered the phrase "prayed up." Yes, I was prayed up. I had been praying consistently about the conference for the past several weeks. I prayed for myself and for the others who would be attending. I knew without a doubt God had made it possible for me to attend this conference. I also knew he had something special planned for me.

I thought about all the things that had prompted me to send that worry email to my friends in the first place. I was worried about my smile showing my crooked not-quite-white teeth. I was concerned about my hair not behaving, worried about using my cane and looking graceless. I was also worried about people rejecting me for being the "rules lady."

My thoughts were interrupted by my daughter Kaitlyn. She popped her head into my office and asked if I would watch her sign the words to the song she was interpreting for a Sunday church service. I waved her in. She put the CD into my player. I watched as she beautifully signed the words to "Do They See Jesus In Me" by Joy Williams. The words washed over me like a balm. Tears came to my eyes as I listened to the message of the music.

God sent Kaitlyn in at just the right time. It was as if a puzzle piece was dropped into place. The picture was suddenly clear. All my worries had been distracting me from what was really important. It didn't matter what people saw when they looked at my physical body, my crooked teeth, a cane, and my hair complete with strands of gray. What was important was that Jesus lived in my heart. Could he be seen in my not-quite-straight smile?

While listening to the song and watching my daughter's graceful movements I remembered why I had been called to write. Words have power to bring God's message to the hearts of those who need him.

Wasn't my goal to be a reflection of God in everything? I needed to remember my commitment and stop worrying about the external.

I attended the conference. Many times God confirmed that I had no reason to worry about going where he sends me. With Jesus in me, I am never alone on the journey. His love is all that needs to be revealed.

HIM VOGEL SAWYER

Kim is a wife, mother, grandmother, teacher, writer, and speaker. In her Kansas home, Kim enjoys quilting and calligraphy and is an avid reader and writer.

A DIFFERENT ROAD

// **PERFORMED BY KATHY TROCCOLI** //

I've traveled long
I've traveled hard
And stumbled many times along the way
I've bruised my knees a lot
And turned my back on God
And seen his mercy
I've been quick to judge
And slow to learn
So many times I've gotten in the way
I think I know so much
I've questioned God enough
But still he loves me

So now I'll walk a different road
I want to see him there before I even go
I've run ahead and gone too slow
I've got to be still now
Wait upon his will now
This time,
It's gonna be his time

Don't want to live without
The peace that comes to me
When I am by his side
I've known the freedom there
Can't find it anywhere
But in Christ Jesus
I believe he's got a plan
Everything in his time
I may not always understand
Everything in his time
Everything in his time

/// COMPASSIONATE FATHER ///

BY LISA RAMADAN

After the break up of a long-term relationship that I thought would lead to marriage, I felt my carefully planned world crumble. I mourned my loss for weeks until finally, I decided to stop crying and feeling sorry for myself.

To fill the large amount of time on my hands, I decided to try some new things. I volunteered for a new program at my local hospital. My role was to help the siblings of the children who were undergoing various medical procedures. The idea was to have someone focus on the child being ignored due to their sibling's illness.

I was assigned to a five-year-old boy whose younger brother had apraxia, a developmental disease that affects speech. I oftentimes went to the family's home to visit. The closer I became to the family, the more impressed I became with them. It wasn't unusual for the boy's mother to talk about her church. She oftentimes spoke of her faith, too, which seemed to provide her with a sense of comfort. Christian music played constantly in their home. In the beginning, I didn't pay much attention to it.

One day, the boy's mother invited me to go to a church function with her. My past experience with church had been limited. I had prayed for better grades. I also prayed that the boys of my dreams would notice me. This was pretty much the extent of my "Christianity."

I agreed and attended church with the family. I prayed that God would send the Holy Spirit to me. I also asked God to forgive me for my sins. My walk, however, was slow. Even though I had sincerely prayed, I didn't feel the excitement that many people felt at their time of conversion.

In addition, I wasn't ready to make such drastic changes in my life. I was afraid that I could no longer have fun. I loved music. I wondered what type of music I could listen to after making that important decision to follow Christ.

The boy's mother then invited me to go with her to a Women of Faith conference. The thought of a women's Christian conference was frightening. I imagined being totally bored. I accepted, but only because of my friend's sincerity. Once again, God was watching over me and somehow I knew I needed to go.

When the day of the conference arrived, I wasn't excited about going. After hearing the speakers, however, I found they were funny, insightful and inspirational. I was having a great time!

Finally, the time came for the musical entertainment. I thought it would be dull. I enjoyed Kathy Troccoli's music more than I could have ever imagined, however. I purchased a CD following her performance. It totally changed my life.

Kathy's first two songs on the album gave me insight into the Christian life that I hadn't anticipated. The first line of "A Different Road" says, "I've traveled long, I've traveled hard and stumbled many times along the way, I've bruised my knees a lot and turned my back on God and seen his mercy." After hearing this line, these thoughts came to my mind, "Kathy Troccoli turned her back on God? But she is a Christian. Shouldn't she simply accept what he gives her and not complain?"

I listened closely to the next line. "I've been quick to judge and slow to learn, so many times I've gotten in the way, I think I know so much, I've questioned God enough but still he loves me."

"Wow," I thought, "even Kathy Troccoli has judged people and questioned God, but God continues to love her." Even more important to me, at the time, was the fact she wasn't perfect. God apparently did not expect her to be.

For my entire life, I tried to be perfect. One of my greatest problems with becoming a Christian was that I didn't see how I could be perfect. I felt less alone when I heard someone who had been a Christian much longer than me confess that she, too, struggles with life issues.

Along with my perfectionist nature, I also have very little patience with certain issues. The last line in this song says, "I believe he's got a plan, everything in his time, I may not always understand, everything in his time."

Again, God was showing me that he had a plan for me, which I wasn't able to know. This meant I could not always be in control. There was comfort in knowing that God is watching over me. Even though I sometimes want total control and, at times, I struggle with patience, I realized that things will turn out better if I completely trust in God.

The second song spoke to me a little later in my Christian walk. Each time I fell, I became furious with myself. Why couldn't I get beyond one sin and then move on to the next? I was trying to be perfect but in a round-about way. Once again, God spoke to me through Kathy's song "At Your Mercy."

"Here I am again, I've failed you Father I have sinned, I'm sad to see how very weak that I can be." The words meant a great deal to me, as they were my thoughts exactly! If Kathy found herself in that situation, other Christians must feel weaknesses, as well.

Although I attended church, Bible studies, classes, and taught Sunday school, I didn't discuss my faith with many other believers. It was encouraging to know, however, that other people struggled, as well.

The next line in the song went like this. "I know I grieve your heart so much, I'm overwhelmed that you still care for me, and I don't want to wander from the truth, Oh God, why do I do the things I do." God still cares for us. He knows that we will continue to sin until we take our last breath. I wondered, "Why do we do the things we do?"

We were born into a sinful world. Only Jesus, a perfect man could save us from our sins. Dying on the cross for us was the ultimate sacrifice. It is hard to imagine a love so great. God loved us so much that he gave his Only Son. Knowing this truth causes me to strive to be a better person. I will never be perfect, but I will try to be the best I can be. I know that the Christian walk is a process. While we are not all walking on the same road at the same time, we should all be striving to move forward.

The end of the song sums up the Christian life. "Satan is a liar, I know he can start a fire, then go tearing everything I have apart, and there's nothing that can take your love away, oh dear Lord, all that I know to do is pray."

I am never certain where the next fire will be or what challenge will be ahead, but I do know that God will love me forever. If I pray as I should God will be there for me.

These songs influenced my walk and my understanding of Christianity. These songs provided insight, comfort, and relief for me. God provides for all of our needs even when we don't understand what our needs are. God is our compassionate and loving Father.

LISA RAMADAN

Lisa is a member of the North Jersey Christian Writers Group. Lisa's interests include teaching children, reading mysteries and cooking.

VICTORY IN JESUS

// WRITTEN BY EUGENE MONROE BARTLETT, SR. //

I heard an old, old story
How a Savior came from glory.
How he gave his life on Calvary
To save a wretch like me.
I heard about his groaning
Of his precious blood's atoning.
Then I repented of my sins
And won the victory!

Chorus:
Oh victory in Jesus!
My Savior forever.
He sought me and bought me
With his redeeming blood.
He loved me ere I knew him
And all my love is due him.
He plunged me to victory
Beneath the cleansing flood.

I heard about his healing
Of his cleaning power revealing.
How he made the lame to walk again
And caused the blind to see.
And then I cried, "Dear Jesus,
Come and heal my broken spirit."
I then obeyed his blest command
And gained the victory.

Chorus

I heard about a mansion
He has built for me in glory.
And I heard about the streets of gold
Beyond the crystal sea.
About the angels singing
And the old redemption story.
And some sweet day I'll sing up there
The song of victory!

/// VIC-TOE-WEE IN JEE-ZUS ///

BY LORI THOMPSON

With eyes the color of milk chocolate, round cherubic cheeks, and short blonde pig tails sticking straight out from the side of her head, my niece sat beside me on one of the back pews at church. With the exception of a few polite "hellos," we went mostly unnoticed. Just because I loved spending time with Nikki I had taken her to my church for the evening services.

Before the concept of Children's Church, nothing beat a large purse filled with Bible storybooks, paper, crayons, toys, gum and a few pieces of candy. My sister and I learned the Girl Scout motto early, "Always be prepared." Being prepared has never been more important than it does during church services with small children.

Nikki was well occupied and seemed unaware of anything going on around her. We had successfully made it through the standard opening song, the prayer, three hymns, and the entire sermon. It was time for the hymn of invitation. While everyone in the building rose to their feet, Nikki remained seated with her head down. She was concentrating on the masterpiece she was coloring.

The song leader led our two hundred member, non-instrumental congregation in the hymn "Victory in Jesus." With her head still down and while she was still coloring, Nikki sang in a voice so deep and raspy that any adolescent boy would have been envious;

> I hood an owd owd sto-wee, how a sa-vyo came fwum glo-wee
> How he gave his wife on cow-va-wee, to save a wetch wike me

Several rows of people turned around to look at us. When they spotted the toddler singing and coloring her picture, their faces nodded in approval with chuckles and smiles.

Nikki continued with the rest of the verse:

I hood about his gwo-ning, of his pwe-shus bwuds a-tone-ing,
Den I we-pen-tid of my sin and won da vic-toe-wee!

By this time, I was trying to suppress my giggling. Much attention was being focused in our direction. I felt proud that my beautiful, tenderhearted niece knew every word to this song. Of course, Nikki couldn't fully comprehend every word she was singing, but her enthusiasm went beyond simple memorization.

As the chorus began, Nikki stopped coloring. Throwing her head back, and in her loudest voice possible, she passionately belted out the words. She sang off-key and one octave below the song leader.

Oh vic-toe-wee in Jee-zus, my say-vyo fo-wev-u,
He sot me and bot me wif his we-dee-meen bwud.
He wuved me ere I knew him, and aww my wuv is dew him,
He pwunged me to vic-toe-wee be-knee da quin-zing fwud.

From every corner, front to back, heads were turning and all eyes were searching for the source of the "melodious" rendition. The song leader stood on his tip-toes while craning his stubby neck. He was attempting to see who was responsible for throwing the congregation out of tune. He was unable to find the face that matched the voice. The adorable blonde toddler was seated with her feet straight out in front of her. She was hidden by the standing congregation. Pacing across the front of the sanctuary, the song leader continued stretching during the remainder of the song.

By this time, my shoulders were shaking. I was doing all I could to muffle my laughter. I am certain that I was several shades of red. Tears were streaming down my face. Never in my entire life have I ever been so out of control in church. I certainly didn't want to do anything to distract Nikki or cause her to stop singing. Nikki was completely unaware that she had attracted so many people's attention.

Red faced with determination, she continued with verse two.

I hood about his he-wing, of his quin-zing pow we-vee-wing
How he made da wame to wok again, and cause da-bwind to see

And den I cwied, dea Jee-zus, come and heaw my bwo-ken spi-wit
I den o-bayd hiz bwest com-mand and gained da vic-toe-wee!"

How could one small child not miss a single beat or skip one word of
a song that many adults, after years of repetition can't even get right?
Maybe her singing wasn't grammatically perfect or on key, but she was
out-singing every person in the place! And above all she was singing
from her heart. There was a meaning in these words that had long
evaded me. I didn't know how much more of this I could stand. My
chest felt like it was going to burst.

During the second chorus, the whispers and snickers continued, as
Nikki sang at full volume. For those who couldn't see her, the word had
gotten to them as to what was causing the disturbance. The only one
who seemed truly frustrated by the experience was the song leader,
who still couldn't see what was happening. I thought he would end the
song there, but he continued with the third verse as well.

Nikki was still praising God with all of her heart.

I hood about a man-shun he has bilt fo me in glo-wee.
I hood about da stweet a gode, be-yon da qui-stal sea.
A-bout de an-gel sing-ing, and de owed we-dim-shun sto-wee,
And some sweet day I sing up dare, da song of vic-toe-wee!

Somehow, I think when the people in the church heard those words
coming from that little child, the song took on an entirely new
meaning. They began singing the chorus with renewed fervor, yet
amazingly they never drowned her out!

O victory in Jesus, my Savior forever.
He sought me and bought me, with his redeeming blood.
He loved me ere I knew him, and all my love is due him.
He plunged me to victory beneath the cleansing flood.

That sweet moment occurred twenty-five years ago. I was only
nineteen. At the time, I was struggling to live the Christian life, and
stay on the right path. I believe God gave me that moment for more
than just a good laugh. He gave me that moment for a lifetime. There
was nothing profound about the event, but it profoundly affected me.

In chapter 10 of the book of Mark, we read about parents bringing their children to Jesus so he could touch them. When the disciples rebuked them for it, Jesus responded indignantly and said, "Let the little children come to me, and do not hinder them, for the kingdom of God belongs to such as these. I tell you the truth, anyone who will not receive the kingdom of God like a little child will never enter it" (Mark 10:14-15, NIV).

The passage ends with these words. "And he took the children in his arms... and blessed them" (Mark 10:16, NIV).

As parents, we should all be eager to bring our children to Jesus and to be touched by him. Nikki was touched by Jesus through her parents' example, and in the learning of that song. In turn, at three and a half years old, Nikki was an example to me. She demonstrated perfectly what it is to receive the kingdom of God like a little child.

God has allowed me to learn numerous lessons through children. Thankfully, we are never too old to learn, or too young to teach.

LORI THOMPSON

Lori has been married twenty-two years and is the mother of two adult sons. She currently works as a secretary for the city school system. She was introduced to Jesus at a young age by wonderful Christian parents and is blessed to know him as her Savior.

IF GOD DIDN'T CARE

// WRITTEN BY LEE ROY ABERNATHY AND HAROLD BARLOW //

We wouldn't have strength to bear our sorrow
If God didn't care
There never would be a glad tomorrow
If God didn't care
We wouldn't have a hope of earning a mansion in the sky
We wouldn't expect our Lord's returning
For if he came and didn't care
He'd surely pass you by
Those welcoming bells would not be ringing
If God didn't care
Those Heavenly voices wouldn't be singing
If God didn't care
He wouldn't have said we'd be rewarded
And promised us joy beyond compare
No, there wouldn't be any hope of Heaven
If God didn't care.

GOD STILL CARES

BY LOUISE MOHORN

my husband looked like nothing but skin and bones as he lay in the hospital bed in our bedroom. Since he become confined to the bed a year earlier, he had deteriorated before my eyes. Gone was the strong man who had protected and provided for me. He was never a man of many words, but now his communication had been reduced to grunts, groans, and wide-eyed stares.

He had been diagnosed with Alzheimer's a few short years earlier. I started noticing the symptoms a few months before he retired, but I convinced myself he was simply exhausted and ready to retire.

We had made big plans after his retirement. Since we had been married, we had always taken care of someone.

We took care of my father first when he was ill. Then we took care of our children. Before they were all out of the house, our first grandchild was born. I took care of him while my daughter worked.

We had decided that after my husband retired, we were going to simply take care of ourselves. We would drive across country, in no hurry to get home. We would take our time and explore each and anything we pleased. We would visit relatives and reminisce about old times.

I knew something wasn't right, however. My husband wasn't acting like himself. He had become forgetful and began doing things outside of his character.

When the diagnosis was made, I felt like my whole world was collapsing. Alzheimer's was something that happened to other people. It couldn't be happening to my husband.

A year after the initial diagnosis came, we received another dread diagnosis. The doctor said the cancer was untreatable and that we should let it run its course.

The days jumbled together in my mind. I suddenly had to do things I had never done before. The car became a burden. Every day household chores became a headache. Things as simple as cutting the grass or moving furniture became a reminder of the loss of simpler days gone by.

Even harder than those things was watching the man I loved—my best friend—whither way.

I squeezed my husband's fragile hand and felt tears spring to my eyes. Where was God? Didn't he care about how much I hurt?

That night, when I was sure my husband was asleep I sat in my recliner and turned on the television. I was trying to unwind. I half-listened to the music playing on a Gaither special. The day had been long and I was growing weary.

As I drifted in and out of sleep, the words to a song captured my attention. The song was called "If God Didn't Care." The end of the song stated:

> Those heavenly voices wouldn't be singing
> If God didn't care
> He wouldn't have said we'd be rewarded
> And promised us joy beyond compare
> No, there wouldn't be any hope of heaven
> If God didn't care

The words reminded me that without God's love in my life, I couldn't get through each day. I realized that even though life was hard, God gives me hope. His love would surround me, though at times it was hard to feel.

God did care. He cared enough to let me know my husband still loved me. Whenever I leaned my cheek toward him, he would kiss it, even though he couldn't speak. I learned to seek joy in the small things. No, God had never left me. He was still there and he still cared about me.

When my husband passed away on October 2, 2002, the song came back to me. The first line reminded me of God's strength, as it stated:

We wouldn't have the strength to bear our sorrow If God didn't care

Even though life was hard I knew I would get through it with God. Even better, was the reminder that one day I would be reunited with my husband. One day, we would be together again. We would take all of those trips that we had planned to take after his retirement.

Instead of marveling at the wonder of the Grand Canyon, we would marvel at the streets of gold. Instead of visiting Old Faithful in Yellowstone, we would admire heavenly mansions and the pearly gates. But most importantly we would be together once again in heaven.

I hold on to that hope and try to remember that God does truly care.

LOUISE MOHORN

Louise lives in Chesapeake, Virginia. She enjoys spending time with her grandchildren and doing anything creative, such as painting, sewing, or gardening. Louise also helps others who are ill and receiving hospice care.

HE TOUCHED ME

// PERFORMED BY BILL GAITHER //

Shackled by a heavy burden
Neath a load of guilt and shame
Then the hand of Jesus touched me
And now I am no longer the same

He touched me, oh he touched me
And oh the joy that floods my soul
Something happened and now I know
He touched me and made me whole

Since I met this blessed savior
Since he cleansed and made me whole
I will never cease to praise him
I'll shout it while eternity rolls

He touched me oh he touched me
And oh the joy that floods my soul
Something happened and now I know
He touched me and made me whole

/// THE TOUCH OF JESUS ///

BY LUCY NEELEY ADAMS

It all started with a routine tummy ache. Our son, Scotty, was resting on the living room couch when my husband, Woody, left home for an out-of-town trip. We thought Scotty would be fine after his stomach ache subsided. But it did not subside.

I rushed Scotty to the hospital and stood by his bedside as the nurses prepared him for an emergency appendectomy. Once we were alone and before he was to be wheeled into the operating room, I searched the Bible beside his bed for some passages that would comfort him. All I could think of was Psalm 100, "Make a joyful noise unto the Lord" (KJV). At that point I had no idea why I was to make any noise to the Lord, much less a joyful one. I prayed with my son. I felt my words only went as far as the ceiling and then fell to the floor.

Even though I had been reared in a church, I lacked any nurture in the faith. I was baptized when I was ten years old and graduated from Bible college. I only had "college knowledge" in my mind, which had not penetrated my heart. I knew about Jesus, but I did not know Jesus. In the hospital room that day, I knew I needed to know Jesus more than ever before. I needed his strength and his guidance. Mostly, however, I needed his peace.

I held back my tears. I wanted my son to think I was strong. I also felt that if I showed strength it would help Scotty to be more courageous. After kissing his soft cheek and stroking his blond hair, he was wheeled into surgery.

"Where is my dear husband?" I wondered. He had received word about the emergency at home, but he was quite a distance away. It would take him several more hours before he could get to us.

What would I do without him? My needs were so pressing. He was the one to whom I always took every burden. I was secure under his care and guidance.

The waiting room looked comforting. Red plaid sofas offered cozy resting places. The bookcase was inviting as I searched for something to pass the time. I found a book that detailed the author's adventures in prayer. She wrote about how God had touched her life time and time again.

I suddenly entered into a new chapter of my life. It dawned on me after reading several of her stories, that I did not know a God in the way she knew him. Was prayer a conversation, followed by the listening for the response of a living God? This was too good to be true. The revelation created a sense of sadness in my heart. Why had I waited so long to want more of God?

That day in a hospital waiting room, I uttered the most exciting prayer of my life. I told God about my deep need. I explained how I realized that no one could fill the empty spaces inside of me except him.

"Oh Lord," I began very slowly as if I wondered if he could hear me, "I do not know you, but I want to. I ask you to help me. Please help me."

As I reflect back on that prayer, I realize that those are the kinds of prayers that God cherishes most. He already knew my heart, but he wanted me to share my feelings and to ask for his help. God answers our sincere prayers when we have the desire to grow closer to him.

God spoke to me that day. I received the good news that Scotty was out of surgery. Everything was fine, and I went right into his room. Scotty was a little groggy, so I sat quietly by his bed and gently patted his hand.

When my husband walked through the door, I witnessed another joyful sight. He had hurried as quickly as he could when he got my phone call asking him to meet us at the hospital. The surgery was short and he had missed the whole thing. We hugged and I cried tears of relief.

I went through the entire ordeal without my husband. I think God had me just where he wanted me, since I usually sat back and let Woody take care of details during emergencies. God knew I needed to weather this storm alone. Otherwise, I may have missed the chance to rely only on the strength of God.

The next few days went well. Scotty continued to heal after we returned home. We attended church the following Sunday. The music was glorious. Even though I had always cherished my piano and choir work, I discovered that I had not taken notice of the lyrics before. This particular Sunday, however, the lyrics rang out clearly in my heart.

Suddenly, each old hymn was like a new declaration to my hungry soul. The truth that kept coming to me was, "Lucy, you are not alone in your search for a deeper faith. Each of these composers expressed the same longings and joys that you are experiencing."

Life went on, but not like usual. I had found a friend in Jesus. His spirit filled my soul and life was sweeter and more peaceful than ever before. I knew Jesus was real. I could express my love through my prayers and have the assurance that he heard every word.

My Bible came alive. I responded to these ancient words as if they were a recent love letter to me, from my Lord. As I read the Gospel accounts of Jesus touching and healing others, I was aware of the mighty truth of the song, "He Touched Me."

Lines from the song reflected my life. "Since I met this blessed Savior, since he cleansed me and made me whole. I will never cease to praise him. I'll shout it while eternity rolls."

That day in the hospital, Jesus truly touched me. He opened my eyes to my need for him. Though I had praised him outwardly, I had never known the true joy of worship. Now that I knew of his presence in my life, I would never cease to praise him. I knew Jesus had touched me and that I would never be the same again.

LUCY NEELEY ADAMS

Lucy and her husband live at Lake Junaluska, North Carolina, where they met and married fifty years ago. They have four children and fourteen grandchildren. Lucy created the radio program "The Story Behind the Song." Her newspaper column "Song Stories" ran for six years in Cookeville, Tennessee and Waynesville, North Carolina.

BE NOT AFRAID

// **WRITTEN BY BOB DUFFORD** //

Chorus:
Be not afraid. I go before you always.
Come follow me, and I will give you rest.

You shall cross the barren desert but you shall not die of thirst.
You shall wander far in safety though you do not know the way.
You shall speak your words in foreign lands and all will understand.
You shall see the face of God and live.

Chorus

If you pass through raging waters in the sea, you shall not drown.
If you walk amid the burning flames, you shall not be harmed.
If you stand before the power of hell and death is at your side,
Know that I am with you through it all.

Chorus

Blessed are your poor, for the kingdom shall be theirs.
Blest are you that weep and mourn, for one day you shall laugh.
And if wicked tongues insult and hate you all because of me,
Blessed, blessed are you.

Chorus

/// NO FEAR ///

BY MARIA FRANZETTI

After being separated from my husband for five years, I asked him for a heart-to-heart talk. I felt that our separation was causing irreparable harm to both of our children. Christopher, our seven year old, had begun a pattern of bad behavior. In a moment of honesty, he blurted out, "I wanted to be so bad that only Daddy could control me. Then he would have to come home."

Living apart from the father they loved so much, and the whirlwind of separate schedules, was just becoming too difficult for all of us. I hoped we could reach some understanding, which would allow my husband to return home. Under counseling, I felt we could become a family again.

What I did not expect to hear was that my husband had been living with another woman for two years. How could he have lived with someone for that long without me knowing? Maybe, I simply did not want to find out.

Over the course of the next week and after much discussion over the telephone, it became clear to me that he could not renounce the other relationship. Reconciliation was not an option if what I wanted was a true relationship. No reconciliation can occur unless both partners put aside all other relationships prior to the attempt to reconcile.

I sat in my kitchen one Wednesday night, after my children realized that the situation was irreparable. We were all devastated, each in our own way. I felt betrayed, confused, angry, and, ironically guilty. My children felt immense pain. I was in too much pain myself to focus on either of them.

So there we sat, attempting to maintain the facade of "dinner." My daughter's face showed the anguish she was feeling. Even at the age of eleven, she felt betrayed, for she had once had a loving bond with her father. She had maintained that bond even though he only saw them once a week. My son was too little to see all the implications, but he felt guilty because his plan had failed to get his father home. In fact, he believed in his heart that his misbehavior had caused the whole situation to explode.

I decided right then and there that we would not stay at home that weekend. It would be too painful to await their dad's Sunday visit and then pretend that all was well. The thought of what those Sundays had meant for five years, with his other life on the side, was revolting. We decided to break the tradition, at least for this Sunday, and take a trip. A flight seemed as good a plan as any at that moment.

I called my cousin, who lived in Rochester (about 250 miles from NY City where we lived). Without giving her many details, I asked if we could spend the weekend with her family. She readily agreed and was a very gracious hostess. Her family was as surprised by this development as we were. In an ironic turn, my husband and I had introduced my cousin and her husband. They had subsequently married as a result of that introduction. So, as a friend and relative, they were both sorry and hurt regarding the situation.

The nights in Rochester are cold; much colder than in New York. My children slept in one spare bedroom and I slept in another. I remember waking up in the middle of the night feeling the chill in the air. It dawned on me that the cold air couldn't come close to the chill I felt inside, as I tried to envision what the future held for me. Even though I had played the role of a single mother for five years, this turn of events seemed more permanent. I could not rely any longer on the hope that this situation was temporary or that all would work itself out. That hope was gone. I faced a new reality, which terrified me.

We attended church with my cousin. We sat in the back. I quietly prayed and cried throughout most of the service. I don't remember much about the worship service. I don't think, even at that moment, I really heard anything being said. My children sat quietly beside me. The sadness in their faces made the situation even worse.

Only twice in my life have I experienced a sheer terror which caused me to lose my breath, feel heart palpitations, and cause me to sweat.

This was the first of those two experiences. I did not want to face reality with my two children who needed me to be strong. At that moment, I did not feel strong.

I prayed a most sincere prayer. "Dearest Lord," I prayed, "you cannot leave me in this condition to face next week. I cannot make it through. You have to give me something to hold on to, or I won't make it."

The organist announced that the final hymn was "Be Not Afraid." I had never heard that particular hymn before. In that moment, however, I knew that this would be the answer to my prayer. I quickly turned to the page in the hymnal. I cried as I read the words "Be not afraid, I go before you always. Come, follow Me, and I will give you rest."

Not only during the next few weeks, but also for many years, I have repeated the words to that hymn over and over in my mind. I truly believe that in that church, on that day, the Lord spoke to me through music.

It is said that the Lord reaches us any way he can. In my life, both prior to that day and since, I had always used music to soothe, uplift and rejuvenate my soul. In times of stress, I responded to music. In hindsight, it is not surprising that God would choose music as his vehicle to respond to my plea for help.

Over the years, during other difficult times, that same hymn has been played at church. Many times, it seems that it was chosen just for me to meet the crisis of the moment and for me to remember the courage the hymn had inspired the first time I heard it. I was changed that day. Though the problems did not go away, I was able to face them. And through the assistance of supportive people, who found their way into my life, I was able to survive. I was also able to provide a home for my two children, the greatest blessings that God had ever given me.

MARIA FRANZETTI

Maria was born and raised in Brooklyn, New York. She currently works as a project manager at an insurance company. She has been blessed with two wonderful children and four beautiful grandchildren. She is an active member in her church.

GREAT IS THY FAITHFULNESS

// WRITTEN BY THOMAS O. CHISHOLM //

Great is Thy faithfulness, O God my Father;
There is no shadow of turning with Thee;
Thou changest not, Thy compassions, they fail not;
As Thou hast been, Thou forever will be.

Chorus:
Great is Thy faithfulness!
Great is Thy faithfulness!
Morning by morning new mercies I see.
All I have needed Thy hand hath provided;
Great is Thy faithfulness, Lord, unto me!

Summer and winter and springtime and harvest,
Sun, moon and stars in their courses above
Join with all nature in manifold witness
To Thy great faithfulness, mercy and love.

Chorus

Pardon for sin and a peace that endureth
Thine own dear presence to cheer and to guide;
Strength for today and bright hope for tomorrow,
Blessings all mine, with ten thousand beside!

Chorus

/// GOD'S FAITHFULNESS ///

BY MARY CONNEALY

As I waited with my family at the gate, I nervously fumbled with the ticket in my hands. It was my first airplane ride. As the wife of a farmer and the mother of four daughters, I had stayed busy at home much of the past twenty-four years. Oftentimes, our family had taken short trips together, such as camping trips to our favorite lake in Minnesota. None of the trips we took, however, required us to fly.

My husband had recently sold all of our cows. With nothing to keep us at home, we decided to visit his mother in Texas. As I waited to board the plane, I thought the butterflies in my stomach might carry me away. They seemed a better option than the 757 waiting outside.

My daughters tried to reassure me that I would be fine. They were old pros when it came to heading for the clouds. Not me, however. Flying was an idea that hadn't quite taken off in my mind.

The attendant called my seat number for boarding. Gripping my ticket, I hesitantly walked through the tunnel leading to the plane. I found my seat, nestled into it, and closed my eyes. I had to make sure my soul was right with the Lord. I assumed that I would die during this flight; therefore I wanted to be ready to meet Jesus. Falling to the earth in an airplane wasn't exactly how I wanted my life to end. At only 47 years of age, I didn't expect to walk through the pearly gates, but I had to be prepared – just in case.

"Lord, be with us," I prayed silently. I gripped the armrest as if I was trying to hold the plane together. I reminded myself that planes took off and landed every day.

"Great Is Thy Faithfulness" is both mine and my father's favorite hymn. I began meditating on the words in the song as the plane neared take-off: "Great is thy faithfulness, oh God my Father. There is no shadow of turning with thee. All I have needed thy hand hath provided. Great is thy faithfulness, Lord unto me."

I sang it silently to myself. With each verse, I examined the words. I found myself still trying to hold the plane up with prayer and a firm grip. The phrase that settled in my heart as the engines fired up was the line, "Great is thy faithfulness, Lord unto me." I had never thought about God being faithful to me in quite that way before. Isn't it my job to be faithful to God?

I began to understand that God is more faithful to us than we could ever be to him. That thought was a blessing to me. I sat there, trying to remember all of my sins so I could ask God to forgive me for them. When I meet Jesus I wanted to be washed as white as snow. I knew that God would be faithful to keep the promises he made to me—to save me and to give me eternal life. I am completely unworthy, but Jesus had covered my unworthiness with his own blood.

"There is no shadow of turning with thee." That is God. He never changes. He is always faithful. "All I have needed thy hand hath provided." Praise the Lord for that precious promise. He is faithful to provide everything that I have ever needed.

I realized that what I needed more than anything else was a personal relationship with Jesus Christ. That song, speaks of all the hope we need to be able to fully give ourselves to God the Father.

That hymn changed my life, as I flew on an airplane. An old hymn I had heard a hundred times before took on a much deeper meaning. It caused my faith in God to grow richer and dearer. Great is Thy Faithfulness, Lord unto me.

MARY CONNEALY

Mary is a wife and the mother of four daughters, Josie, Wendy, Shelly, and Katy. She is employed by the Lyons Mirror-Sun, her hometown newspaper, for which she writes a weekly book review column.

TOUCH OF THE MASTER'S HAND

// PERFORMED BY WAYNE WATSON //

Well it was battered and scarred
And the auctioneer felt it was hardly worth his while
To waste much time on the old violin, but he held it up with a smile
Well, it sure ain't much, but it's all we got left
I guess we ought to sell it
Oh, now who'll start the bid on this old violin?
Just one more and we'll be through

And then he cried one give me one dollar
Who'll make it two only two dollars who'll make it three
Three dollars twice now that's a good price
Now who's gonna bid for me?
Raise up your hand now don't wait any longer the auctions about to end
Who's got four Just one dollar more to bid on this old violin?

Well the air was hot and the people stood
Around as the sun was setting low
From the back of the crowd a gray-haired man
Came forward and picked up the bow
He wiped the dust from the old violin then he tightened up the strings
Then he played out a melody pure and sweet
Sweeter than the Angels sing
And then the music stopped and the auctioneer
With a voice that was quiet and low he said now what am I bid
For this old violin and he held it up with a bow.

And then he cried out one give me one thousand
Who'll make it two only two thousand who'll make it three
Three thousand twice you know that's a good price
Common who's gonna to bid for me?
And the people cried out what made the change we don't understand
Then the auctioneer stopped and he said with a smile
It was the touch of the Master's hand.

You know there's many a man with his life out of tune
Battered and scared with sin and he's auctioned cheap
To a thankless world much like that old violin
Oh, but then the Master comes
And that old foolish crowd they never understand
The worth of a soul and the change that is rough
Just by one touch of the Masters hand.

And then he cried out one give me one thousand
Who'll make it two only two thousand who'll make it three
Three thousand twice you know that's a good price
Common who's gonna bid for me?
And the people cried out what made the change we don't understand
Then the auctioneer stopped and he said with a smile
It was the touch, that's all it was; it was the touch of the Master's hand
It was the touch of the Master's hand; oh, it was the touch of the Master's hand.

Words by James N. Miller and Mira Brooks Welch. © 1976 Paragon Music Corp.
ASCAP Portions of text © Brethren Press, Elgin, IL, used by permission of Benson
Music Group.

/// GOD'S MASTERPIECE ///

BY MICHELLE "MIKE" BURCHER

I could tell by the tight expression on my friend's face that she wasn't happy. Sternness lined her eyes. Her mouth was pulled into a tight line.

"We need to talk," she said.

I had no idea what was going on. My friends and I were simply enjoying another night at college. We had all been chatting, doing nothing out of the ordinary. As I looked at my friend's face, a feeling of dread settled in my stomach. I braced myself for whatever she had to say.

"Do you love me?" my friend asked.

The question took me by surprise. "Of course I love you," I said. "I would die for you."

She looked me in the eye. "No, you don't. You can't love me because you don't love yourself. Jesus says love your neighbor as yourself. You have no idea what it means to love yourself, therefore you cannot possibly love me."

A slap couldn't have stung any worse. But I realized there was truth in her words. All night long I had been putting myself down. My self-esteem was low. With the hope of helping me, my friend was quick to point out the flaw.

I had grown up as an only child. My parents regularly fought. We had moved quite a bit. Since I was always the new kid on the block other kids picked on me. After hearing others say that I was ugly, stupid, or bad, I began to believe them.

By the time I reached junior high, I didn't think very highly of myself. I came to a point in my life where I just decided not to make friends. It was too hard being around other people. I built barriers between other people and myself. Since I didn't like myself, I made sure that nobody else liked me either.

Between the seventh and eighth grade, our family moved again. A girl down the street invited me to youth group. I didn't want to go. I figured that if she was brave enough to ask me, however I would go ahead and accept. I found something new at her church. People there wanted to know me. They also asked me what I enjoyed doing. I had never experienced that before.

Youth group was fun. I continued going. They encouraged me by telling me that I had something to offer and by letting me know I was worthwhile to God.

"No, I'm not," I replied. I didn't believe their compliments could possibly be true. Even though I was there, in a positive environment, their words just didn't sink in.

In the tenth grade, I considered going into professional ministry. The associate pastor at my church encouraged me, so I discussed it with my guidance counselor. She laughed in my face when I told her my idea.

"Maybe she was right," I decided. "Why would God want someone like me in the ministry?"

I went to college. I found myself doing the same things many college students do when they are free from adult influence. I was on a path to self-destruction. That was when my friend sat me down and opened my eyes to how I was acting.

Two or three years later while driving, I tuned in to a Christian radio station. I didn't usually pay much attention to the music on the radio. That particular day, however, it was like God reached through the radio and said, "You must listen to this." So I did.

The song, "The Touch of the Master's Hand," came across the airwaves. It is a ballad about an old and shabby violin that went up for auction. No one wanted to bid on it because they didn't think it was worth much. Then an old man stepped forward, tweaked it a bit, and began playing a beautiful song. Afterward, everyone realized how much the instrument was worth.

Through that song, God helped me to understand that my worth didn't come from what I thought about myself. My worth didn't come from what other people thought of me either. My worth came completely from what God thought about me.

I was able to put things into perspective. I recognized that I was valuable and that I had something to contribute, simply because God loved and valued me. God created me, battered and scarred, to become a beautiful instrument for him. God would use me in powerful ways. The call to join the ministry came back to me. I had no excuses. I had to follow God's leading.

As the director of a Christian camp for the past seventeen years, I have the opportunity to tell the story of how God changed me quite a few times. Each week after I sing "The Touch of the Master's Hand," I remind the campers that it doesn't matter what others think of them. It doesn't even matter what they think of themselves. They are worth everything to God, so much that he sent his Son to die for them.

I am asked to tell my story each and every year. Just when I think the listeners would be tired of hearing it, they beg to hear it again. They want to hear that God loves them. They need to know they are valuable to him. They also want to feel the "Touch of the Master's Hand" in their own lives.

MICHELLE "MIKE" BURCHER

Mike has been the Director of Makemie Woods Camp and Conference Center in Virginia since 1992. She and her husband have two children.

THE OTHER SIDE OF THE RADIO

// PERFORMED BY CHRIS RICE //

Here I am on the other side of the radio
Wonderin' why I'm here and why anybody cares what I say
No I'm not a better man cause I'm singing my songs on the radio
Cause were all the same, at the end of the day

Now I imagine you on the other side of the radio
Doin' your homework or driving with your windows down on the freeway
I see you tappin' the wheel I see you bobbin' your head to the radio
Oh and it makes my day, to see that smile on your face
And in some small way, I remember my place

Cause it's you and me singing the same song right now
And maybe this will bring us together somehow
And maybe there's a million people all singing a long
Somebody started thinkin' about the third line
And maybe somebody's saying a prayer for the first time
And that's enough reason to keep me singing my song,
Singing my songs, on the other side of the radio

Crank up the volume sing at the top of your lungs with the radio
Tune it in to some good news and laughing along with the DJ
We're changing someone's world from the other side of the radio
Oh and it makes my day to see that smile on your face
And in some small way, I remember my place

Cause it's you and me singing the same song right now
And maybe this will bring us together somehow
And maybe there's a million people all singing a long
Somebody started thinkin' about the third line
And maybe somebody's saying a prayer for the first time
And that's enough reason to keep me singing my song
Singing my song, on the other side of the radio

BACK TO THE OTHER SIDE OF THE RADIO

BY NANCY TYLER

I yanked the microphone into position and held it just below my desperately dry mouth. It had been 16 years since I had spoken on the radio. As I sat in the studio, I wondered what I was doing.

The "On Air" sign lit up. I realized, with some anxiety, that it was time for me to begin talking.

"Hi, I'm Nancy Tyler. Don't go anywhere. Coming up next—a surprising mix of music—on *True Story* Radio—here on WEBR."

The first song was rolling. It was only six seconds into the show. In two minutes and fifty seconds, I would introduce the song that God used to help get me back on the air: Chris Rice's "The Other Side of the Radio."

When I was eight, I fell in love with broadcasting while hiding in my room listening to the news, wacky morning announcers, and old-time radio comedies on my dad's clock radio. Dad got tired of tracking down his pilfered radio, so we made a deal. I returned his to him. In turn, he gave me my own: a red, white, and blue pocket transistor.

I didn't discover Christian music on that little radio, however. I was introduced to Christian music when my junior high youth pastor insisted that we give up secular music. Once I discovered a couple of fun Christian radio stations, I gladly cut back on my Top 40s habit.

Once I received my driver's license in the mid-1980s, I slipped off to my favorite Christian station outside of Philadelphia. It was a small station, broadcasting only from sunrise to sunset. Preachers took up most of the airtime. I was wild about the music show, however. The mix of songs and the DJ who played them compelled me to listen.

James Martin did not own a booming radio voice. There was an unpolished sweetness about his Philadelphia accent. James had been given the freedom to play what he wanted. He played both current songs and old ones from the "Jesus Movement" days of the 70s. He had a purpose behind his selections. Many times he laced songs together with encouragement, scripture, and fan interviews.

James allowed me to stop by the station often. My heart raced when he handed me the microphone and asked what God was teaching me. He let me choose and introduce various songs, read related Bible verses, and interview music artists.

Not long after I started college in Washington, DC, and began my own Christian radio show on campus, James left the business. And sadly, we lost touch. But I held onto and kept developing a vision for Christian radio, based on what James had taught me.

I intended to go on the air full-time after I graduated. Instead, God led me into a different profession. I managed media productions for a government agency. I burrowed into my career, got married, and was widowed. When I found some old tapes from mine and James's show, God reawakened my love for Christian music.

I made a point of spending time with Christian musicians when they toured the area. I sensed God drawing me into Christian music more deeply, as he created opportunities for me to minister to the artists who created the music, and also to the fans who loved it.

Chris Rice's label, Rocketown Records, touched my heart. I read about the sacrifices the group made which allowed Chris to focus on youth ministry, his first priority. Like Chris, I wanted to help kids. I also wanted to support the artists who were more dedicated to serving God and creating quality music than to generating big profits.

With time, the label entrusted me to volunteer in helping moderate their message boards. They were populated by the wonderful fans of the label and its artists.

Returning home from church one morning I listened to Chris as he sang about "The Other Side of the Radio." I caught myself doing everything he said in the song. My windows were down. I bobbed my head. I tapped the wheel. And I sang along. In mid-head bob, I realized that I missed doing Christian radio. Suddenly, I had to get back there.

I found a community station, which trained volunteers to produce and host their own shows. I sat in front of the mixer board, with my headphones on and the microphone in place. I felt more at home in that studio than I had felt anywhere in a long time.

After years of losses, discouragements, but also with many with wonderful memories, I went back to radio. Just as I had changed, Christian music had changed, as well. I can play rock and punk, hip-hop, R&B, and bluegrass with high quality words and music, and not showcase half of what Christian music offers today.

Radio has changed greatly, as well. The tapes I edited with razor blades in college were replaced with records. Records were replaced by computers, which now allow me to record and edit music digitally.

Just as always, radio is the most intimate form of mass communication. It engages the imagination. Furthermore, Christian music may be the most intimate type of music because it engages the spirit. Christian radio stirs listeners to feel, to think, to encourage their hope in Christ, and to draw them into worship.

There may be a million people singing to Chris Rice's songs all over the world. I could probably name most of *True Story*'s listeners, from the station where God placed me. I have the opportunity to minister to the listeners through songs and chat, Bible passages, and interviews, which make up each week's show.

I am so grateful that God drew me close to him through Christian music on more than one occasion and also from both sides of the radio.

NANCY TYLER

Nancy writes, serves and encourages artists and other people in the Christian music industry. She also counsels and ministers to Christian music fans online. She also hosts *True Story*, the one-hour, weekly Christian music show for WEBR Radio.

AFTER THE MUSIC FADES

// PERFORMED BY SHAUN GROVES //

Lord, take me
From this place
Into a world that has no time.
No hurries, no worries,
Gladly I leave them all behind
Down here; I'm letting go and drawing
near.

I wanna sing.
I wanna fly.
I wanna see from your side of the sky.
I wanna love.
I wanna stay,
Wanna be close to you
Long after the music fades.

Lord, I come
To give you
Much more than just a melody.
Please take me and break me;
Right now God, I don't want to leave
Unchanged; I never wanna be the same.

I wanna sing.
I wanna fly.
I wanna see from your side of the sky.
I wanna love.
I wanna stay,
Wanna be close to you
Long after,

'Cause Lord you are
Mighty, Awesome, Righteous,
Gracious, Knowing,
In me overflowing.
Father, Teacher, Master, Leader
Jealous, Loving, you are.

And you make me wanna sing.
I wanna fly.
I wanna see from your side of the sky.
I wanna love.
I wanna stay,
Wanna be close to you
Long after,

And I wanna sing.
I wanna fly.
I wanna see from your side of the sky.
And I wanna love.
I wanna stay,
Wanna be close to you
Long after,
Wanna be close to you
Forever after,
Wanna be close to you,
Long after the music fades,
Long after the music fades.

/// CHANGE FOR THE FUTURE ///

BY NANCY TYLER

Working two blocks from the White House was exciting. I found importance in the bustle of commuters, the enthusiasm of tourists, and the excitement of motorcades. But on September 11, 2001, the thrill of working close to the White House turned to terror.

That morning, my shocked coworkers and I huddled around the television watching the World Trade Center towers crumble into dust. Rumors of other attacks were false, but a column of smoke rising over the nearby Pentagon was real. And so was the report that one more plane was still in the sky, possibly heading for the White House.

The phones died while I was leaving a message for my mom to let her know that I was "safe." But with the threat of a plane coming, my coworkers and I struggled to decide whether we should stay in our office or try to get home. I kept thinking: "I have to explain the Gospel one more time to as many people in this office as I can." So I prayed hard and did my best. And then we headed home.

The subway was closed, so I waited for a coworker to navigate his car out of a mobbed parking garage and onto the jammed street. A coworker, whose fiancé was in the burning Pentagon, was with me. Another was concerned that she may be going into premature labor. A group of heavily armed Secret Service agents ordered us to get off the street and under cover until our ride arrived.

It took nearly two hours to go eight miles where our own vehicles were parked at a subway station. I looked up numbly at the golden sunlight and royal blue sky, just before I got into my car. It was one of the most beautiful days I could remember. I could see the beauty of the day, but couldn't find joy in it.

I wasn't interested in listening to music, but when I turned the key, a

CD by Shaun Groves began playing. I focused on the lyrics of "After the Music Fades" for the first time. The words echoed in my mind: "Right now God, I don't want to leave unchanged."

Once home, I rolled up in a blanket and stayed there for a day and a half. I forgot to eat. I watched the images of crashing planes and rubble and flames over and over again. I turned to television stations that didn't normally carry news. I stared at the test patterns and condolence messages to America on the screen.

Two days later, I returned to work. I emerged from the subway to eerily empty and barricaded streets. Busloads of troops and military vehicles were the only traffic that could be seen. In the following weeks, we dealt with bomb scares, and anthrax was found in my building.

I tried my best to "let go and draw near" to God, but I felt so off balance. After years of being involved in college, church, and community ministries, I was used to being the encourager. I was the one who looked after everybody else. But now I needed someone to look after me. Fear and questions about the future shook me. I sat in the dark at night crying out to a seemingly silent God. I immediately wanted to leave Washington.

Even before September 11, I realized that DC didn't seem to be the best fit for me any longer. I was a young widow. I was tired of working for the government and hungry for change. But God hadn't opened any opportunities for me to make a move. Right up to that September morning, I impatiently wrestled with God over it.

It was hard for me not to just leave, regardless of whether or not God was doing the leading. But he helped me hold on. God helped me to see his side. People in DC, for whom I had been praying finally wanted to talk about Christ. As I prayed the line from the song: "I wanna be close to you long after the music fades," I felt the hope in me rising. My hope was revealed in my journal entries: "9.23.2001: All the lights are on in all the little houses on my street. A fighter jet flies very low overhead. It constantly traces its pattern, as if it is protecting the houses. The bass in my stereo kicks on. The floor shakes. I have to stop to decide if it's the music rumbling the floorboards or if something bad has happened outside. I have not fully recovered from September 11. I hope I never will."

I caught myself returning to my "woe be to me" rants. God had not given me all the things I told him I wanted. The clay again calls the master potter slow and untalented.

I don't want to slink around in angry frustration for being where I don't want to be and doing what I don't want to do anymore. I pray and evaluate my heart. I realize that I am meant to stay right where I am.

I stand in a shower of exploded dreams and feel alone. But still, I have to be in this place. I think of the loved ones at my job, at my church, and in my neighborhood. I am compelled to be right here, right now.

Going anywhere else at this time would be cowering from the call. Going somewhere safe, to avoid the terror, is to go somewhere that could quench the purpose of my life. Everything I thought mattered has disintegrated into a fine dust that covers my landscape.

Since that difficult time, God has given me many opportunities to deepen relationships. I have been able to express my hope in Christ with coworkers and neighbors. Many of these people have entered my life since September 11. God has also allowed me to reach beyond the walls of Washington in an online ministry encouraging and serving fans and professionals in the Christian music industry.

God kept me safe and used me in a place where I didn't want to be. He never left me to fight my fears and frustrations alone, however. September 11 serves as a milestone when I consider my relationship with my Father. It is a reminder that long after the music fades I will still be close to him.

NANCY TYLER

Nancy writes and serves and encourages artists and other people in the Christian music industry. She also counsels and ministers to Christian music fans online. She also hosts *True Story*, the one-hour, weekly Christian music show for WEBR Radio.

ON MY WAY TO YOU

// PERFORMED BY MERCY ME //

Almost there, almost where I'm supposed to be
It's not all clear, but you keep showing me
With every step, the more my heart moves to your beat
Just like where I'm headed, there's joy in the journey

Chorus:
Teach me to think like you think
Show me the things, that are true
Finish the work you have started in me
As I'm on my way to you As I'm on my way to you

Create in me a pure heart and make me new
Less of me, Jesus more of you
Here I stand, still I'm drawn down to my knees
It's not my strength, but Yours that carries me

Chorus

/// THE JOURNEY TO GOD ///

BY REA GRAY

Life had not turned out the way I had expected. I was in my third marriage. I look back today and cringe at the mistakes I made over the years. I find that sometimes, as we seek to find God, the road can be painful.

I called myself a Christian when I was a child. I didn't have a real relationship with God, however. As soon as I began my college career, I started living a pagan lifestyle. At the beginning of my senior year, I met a man in a bar. We moved to New York City and married a year later. In Manhattan, I worked at a large law firm where alcohol, drugs, and infidelity were common.

My husband and I had three wonderful children. But something was still missing in my life. I found myself searching for something to fill the empty places in my heart. I was an exercise fanatic. While I looked great on the outside, I felt empty and angry on the inside.

In the meantime, my husband Scott was busy trying to build the business he had started with a friend. This meant long hours, endless client meetings, and a great deal of time away from home. Scott and I never fought. Unfortunately we never communicated either. We both spent too much time with friends and not enough time with each other. After eleven years of marriage, we divorced.

I became good friends with a younger coworker. She was also a single mom. My new friend and I spent weekends drinking and partying. I was desperately craving attention, participating in self-destructive behavior. I was as far away from God as I had ever been.

Then, one of my son's hockey coaches and I began dating. It wasn't long before I discovered that he had a cocaine addiction. I just knew I could fix him, however. After a tumultuous year of dating, we were married. But the next three years we fought. He moved in and out. I suffered physical and emotional abuse. I lived through serious financial struggles.

At the law firm, I worked with Becky, a wonderful, kind, and patient woman. We went to lunch together every day. She listened attentively to my endless complaining about the horrible life I was living.

Becky was a Christian. She was married to a wonderful and godly man. Becky was compassionate. She cared about everyone. She rode the bus to work hoping she might get the opportunity to witness to other people. She was the most generous person I had ever met, always giving to the needy. Becky never preached to anyone, but because of her caring, kind, and loving actions I recognized Jesus.

I remember driving home from work one day and saying aloud, "I want what Becky has." For the first time I heard God speak to me. He whispered, "You can, my child. Just open your heart and let me in."

Jim was not living at home. My life was a mess, but the kids and I started going to church. God opened my eyes to the fact that he had never left or forsaken me.

On Mother's Day, 1996, I felt the Holy Spirit pull me off the pew and lead me to the front of the church. I completely surrendered my life to him and publicly rededicated my life. I knew God had big plans for me. I wanted to live within his will and receive the blessings of his promises. I wanted my own personal relationship with Jesus Christ.

I knew, too, that God never said we wouldn't go through difficult times. The next few years were very stormy. After receiving a phone call from "the other woman," I was both hurt and angry. At the same time, however, I was relieved to be released from this unhealthy marriage. Unfortunately, I was once again a single parent. This time, however, I would be raising four children alone.

I spent a great deal of time beating myself up over the choices I had made in the past. I regretted the consequences that my children and I were paying. One particular morning, I asked God for forgiveness. For the second time in my life, I heard God's voice very clearly. He said, "I have forgiven you my child. Now you have to forgive yourself." The message from God drastically changed my life.

I knew everything would work out as long as I was faithful and obedient to the Lord. I was in a financial bind. I eventually had to file bankruptcy in order to keep my home. I turned my van back over to the lender which left us without transportation. I continued to tithe, however. Blessings dropped in my lap everywhere I turned. Food and gifts were provided for our family at Christmas, by my small group members. Someone in the group gave me a Geo Metro. I felt like someone just handed me the keys to a brand new Cadillac! I sat down to pay bills, and for the first time in many years, I paid them all. I had ninety-eight cents left over! God became so real to me.

At a Bible study, I met Tom. That night, as we joined hands to pray, it was like electricity flowed between us. We dated for four months and then we were married.

Life continues to have its trials. But, I love the Lord. I enjoy doing what God calls me to do as wife and mother. I am certain that everything will work out for the best. Romans 8:28 tells us, "In all things God works for the good of those who love him, who have been called according to his purpose" (NIV).

When I heard the song "On My Way to You" by Mercy Me, I felt like the words could have been written just for me. I made mistakes that I have regretted over the years, but I know God carried me through. Through all the hard times, he was there, calling me back to him.

I wish the past had been different. I realize that I cannot change it, however. I also realize that the pains of my past are the events which took me to a deeper fellowship with my Lord and Savior, Jesus Christ. Instead of mourning over the days gone by, I rejoice daily in my future. I am thrilled that I am on my way to God!

REA GREY

Rea has four children ranging in age from seven to eighteen. She is the preschool director and special event coordinator for Mount Pleasant Christian Church.

FAMILY MAN

// **PERFORMED BY ANDREW PETERSON** //

I am a family man
I traded in my mustang for a mini-van
This is not what I was headed for when
I began
This was not my plan
I am a family man

But everything I had to lose
Came back a thousand times in you
And you fill me up with love
Fill me up with love
And you help me stand
'Cause I am a family man

And life is good
That's something I always knew
But I just never understood
If you'd asked me then, you know I'd say
I never would
Settle down in a neighborhood
I never thought I could

But I don't remember anymore
Who I even was before
You filled me up with love
Filled me up with love
And you help me stand

So come on with the thunderclouds
Let the cold winds rail against us
Let the rain come down
We can build a roof above us with the
love we found
And we can stand our ground
So let the rain come down

'Cause love binds up what breaks in two
So keep my heart so close to you
And I'll fill you up with love
Fill you up with love
And I'll help you stand
'Cause I'm a family man

I'm saving my vacation time for
Disneyland
This is not what I was headed for when
I began
This was not my plan
It's so much better than
So much better than
'Cause I am a family man

/// THE MAN OF THE FAMILY ///

i will never forget the day my wife told me she was pregnant with our first child. An overwhelming joy washed over me. I was finally going to be a dad!

Sometimes it felt surreal. We had been trying for four years and, at times, I wondered if children would ever be a part of our future. As my wife's stomach steadily grew, however, reality embedded itself. I realized this was not a dream.

Along with my excitement came fear. Would I be a good father? Would my baby be healthy? What would the future hold for our family?

My wife and I sorted out our business, trying to get everything in order. I realized that changes and sacrifices needed to be made. My wife would stay at home, which would mean a significant cut in our income. We needed a new computer and car, but those things would have to wait. Although we loved to travel, we wouldn't be able to take a vacation for awhile. Simply spoken, our lives would change drastically.

Before our baby was born, my wife and I went to a Christian concert. Andrew Peterson performed the opening act. I had heard him sing before and really enjoyed his music.

Toward the end of his set, he spoke about a new song from his album, *Love and Thunder*. The song was called "Family Man." He told the story of how he wrote the song for his brand new daughter. Since we were going to have a baby girl, his words grabbed me! As he sang, I could relate to each line. It felt good to know I wasn't alone. Both my fears and joys were common to all.

The song spoke about trading in a Mustang for mini-van and settling down in a neighborhood. I could relate to those words. I even found comfort in them. I was becoming a dad myself. I was ready to make whatever sacrifice needed.

On June 5, 2003 my beautiful daughter, Lauren Nichole Werlinger was born. I held her. Everything I had given up came back to me a million times in her. She filled my heart with love. I have never seen anything more perfect in my entire life.

Three days later, I loaded my family into the car and headed for home. I played "Family Man" the entire way to our house. Tears tracked their way slowly down my cheeks. I was on cloud nine. I knew the sacrifices wouldn't be easy, but worth what I would receive in turn.

"I don't remember anymore, who I even was before," was a phrase in the song that touched me. I gladly embraced the new person I had become. No matter what, I would consider my child. She would not be the center of our lives, however. That was God's sole position. Our daughter was so important to us the sacrifices we had made no longer hurt.

Though my wife and I loved going on cruises, now we were planning a trip to Disneyland. I looked forward to taking my daughter to the Grand Canyon and Niagara Falls, where she could see God's glory. My hopes and dreams have joyfully changed to include Lauren.

Of course, fears sometimes plague me. SID's petrified me. I don't think I slept a full night for over a month just thinking about what could happen. I turned the monitor on high. If I heard a noise I jumped out of bed to go check on her.

I am afraid that I won't discipline her enough. Then I fear that I might discipline her too much. I am sometimes afraid that I won't be a good example for her. I fear that I won't be a good provider. I fear that I will fail to teach her everything she needs to know before she goes into the real world. I fear that I won't shelter her enough. I fear that I will shelter her too much. I simply want my daughter to have the best this world had to offer. I am afraid that I will fail to give it to her.

The lines to the song states, "But I don't remember anymore, who I even was before. You filled me up with love. Filled me up with love and you helped me stand."

I know we will face trials in the future. I know also that thunderclouds and cold winds will come our way. But I also know that our love will sustain us. Our hope will keep us strong. Now, I was a "Family Man."

ſHANE WERLINGER

Shane and his wife have a daughter. Shane works as a computer support technician.

THE ſILENCE OF GOD

// **PERFORMED BY ANDREW PETERSON** //

It's enough to drive a man crazy; it'll break a man's faith
It's enough to make him wonder if he's ever been sane
When he's bleating for comfort from Thy staff and Thy rod
And the heaven's only answer is the silence of God

It'll shake a man's timbers when he loses his heart
When he has to remember what broke him apart
This yoke may be easy, but this burden is not
When the crying fields are frozen by the silence of God

And if a man has got to listen to the voices of the mob
Who are reeling in the throws of all the happiness they've got
When they tell you their troubles have been nailed up to that cross
Then about the times when even followers get lost?
'Cause we all get lost sometimes...

There's a statue of Jesus on a monastery knoll
In the hills of Kentucky, all quiet and cold
And he's kneeling in the garden, as silent as a stone
All his friends are sleeping and he's weeping all alone

And the man of all sorrows, he never forgot
What sorrow he carried by the hearts that he bought
So when the questions dissolve into the silence of God
The aching may remain, but the breaking does not
The aching may remain, but the breaking does not
In the Holy, lonesome echo of the silence of God

/// GOD'S SILENCE ///

BY SHANE WERLINGER

The ringing of the telephone interrupted my family's peaceful afternoon barbecue. My wife, Sandy, answered it. One the other end was her sister, who lived about an hour and a half away from us. Sandy's relaxed demeanor suddenly became rigid. I felt myself become tense, as I sensed the urgency of the phone call.

"What's going on?" I heard my wife ask. "Can you put them on the phone?"

I watched as she listened intently and then hung up the phone.

"The police are at Barb's," Sandy informed me. "They say there had been an accident and Jimmy was most likely involved." Jimmy was Barb's son.

Both people who were riding in the truck had died. The bodies could not be identified because they were burned too badly. They would need dental records to secure absolute proof. From the information the authorities had, however, one of them was probably Jimmy.

I hugged Sandy and tried to offer reassurance. "We don't know anything for sure," I told her.

We packed up our six-week old baby girl and headed to Barb's house. The ride there was fairly silent. We were both praying. I had Andrew Peterson's CD, "*Love and Thunder*," in the player. His song, "The Silence of God," filled the car with haunting words. As the song played I fought back tears.

I had heard it many times before and really liked it. I always thought that I understood the meaning, but on that drive the lyrics took on a brand new meaning. One of the verses talks about the Garden of Gethsemane. Singing about Christ, it says:

And he's kneeling in the garden, as silent as a stone
All his friends are sleeping and he's weeping all alone

The image of my Savior praying before God in the Garden of Gethsemane was an odd comfort. Just as I was pleading out to God, Jesus had done the same.

I asked God to take this cup from my lips, as Christ did two thousand years before. I begged God to let Jimmy to be all right, though in my heart I knew the truth. This song made me realize that though I didn't understand God's will, I needed to trust him in it. At that moment I had to turn it all over to him. I whispered, "Not my will Lord, but Yours."

Sandy ran to her sister the minute we arrived. Barb's wail of agonizing sorrow cut through the night air. I wasn't sure if I could face this burden. I knew I could not do it on my own. I also knew that God would be with me.

We stayed with Barb for a few days. We helped her make proper arrangements and get the information together that was needed. Life seemed like a whirlwind. At times, I felt like I was going crazy. Many times, I needed to get away for a few minutes. I would drive to the store to pick up some groceries or other needed items. While in the car, I listened to "The Silence of God" over and over again.

We all asked the same question. "Why did this have to happen to someone so young? At sixteen, Jimmy's life was just getting started.

Barb moved in with us in September. She got a job to help occupy her time. Sandy and I tried our best to be supportive and help Barb adjust. Things began to return to normal. Then the next blow hit our family.

My dad had some tests run on his liver. He had been sick during recent days. The doctor wanted to make sure everything was okay. Unfortunately, they discovered that Dad had advance liver cancer. He was told to begin hospice care. This came as a shock to all of us.

We thought Dad might be able to fight the disease, but it was too advanced. My dad asked the doctor if he would make it to trout season. The doctor said that was very likely. Though he was sick, I hoped I would have some time to spend with my dad. Unfortunately, that was not the case.

I returned home from a business trip shortly thereafter. Thirty minutes later, I received a phone call from my sister. She told me that my dad was gone. I couldn't believe it. I had seen Dad the last Saturday. At that time, he seemed fine. I realized that I was not ready for this. I drove to my sister's house with my wife and baby. Once again, The "Silence of God" played. Once again, it moved me to tears.

The following week was a blur of events. The lyrics of "The Silence of God" echoed through my head. The song provided a quiet comfort in a time of pain.

> So when the questions dissolve into the silence of God
> The aching may remain, but the breaking does not
> The aching may remain, but the breaking does not
> In the Holy, lonesome echo of the silence of God

I was comforted to know that though I would ache with pain, the breaking would not remain forever.

I continue to miss both my dad and my nephew today. I have asked God many times why these events had to happen. He hasn't given me an answer as of yet. I do have the assurance, however, that God's will is perfect and just.

The Christian life is not always pain free. We are never assured that trouble won't come. We are assured, however, that God will be there to help us through the tough times we face. Our questions will not always be answered. We can have the assurance, however, that the God who created the universe is a perfect and loving God that cares for you and me. If we put our trust in Jesus we can face all the problems we encounter.

ʃHANE WERLINGER

Shane and his wife have a daughter. Shane works as a computer support technician.

LIVE THROUGH ME

// **PERFORMED BY ANNE MACCALLAM** //

I talk about serving but am I servant
I talk about giving but do I sacrifice
I talk about loving but do I hold back
I can lost within myself

I'm supposed to be growing but am I still
a child
I'm supposed to be going but I'm still
here
I'm supposed to be following the Lord
my God
(but) I can get lost within myself

(but) Lord you came to live in me
The day I believed in you
Loving you will bring me to
Live what I believe, live what I believe

You could talk about serving cause you
were a servant
You could talk about giving because you
sacrificed
You could talk about loving, You did not
hold back...

(and) Lord you came to live in me
The day I believed in you
Loving you will bring me to
Live what I believe, live what I believe

That it's not just what I do
But all of who I am
Lord, make me more like you
So you can live on through
This one

Serve through me
Give through me
Love through me
Live through me (repeat)

(cause) Lord you came to live in me
The day I believed in you
Loving you will bring me to
Live what I believe, live what I believe

It's not just what I do but all of who I am
Lord, make me more like you so you can
live on through
This one...

Serve through me...
Give through me...
Love through me...
Live through me...

LETTING GOD LIVE THROUGH ME

/// ///

BY SHELBY ROUNTREE

the weekend getaway had served to renew and refresh my tired and aching spirit. But now I was on my way back to reality. I had recently become a single mother to two young sons. I was preparing to re-enter the workforce, trying to maintain our home, and desperately searching for a sense of security and well-being. I wasn't ready to deal with those problems. I wanted my weekend getaway to take me away from it all.

I slid a CD into the player as I accelerated onto the interstate. My friend gave me the disc on my way out of town, telling me that her church praise team recorded it. She followed by saying she hoped it would bless me.

As the music played, the tone of the guitar echoed throughout my weary heart. The lyrics began:

> I talk about serving, but am I a servant?
> I talk about giving, but do I sacrifice?
> I talk about loving, but do I hold back?
> I can get lost within myself.

The sincerity and gentleness in the singer's voice matched perfectly with the instruments and served as a soothing balm for my raw soul. The song continued:

> I'm supposed to be growing, but am I still a child?
> I'm supposed to going, but I'm still here.
> I'm supposed to be following the Lord my God
> But I can get lost within myself.
> Lord, you came to live in me the day I believed in you.
> Loving you will bring me to live what I believe.

I lifted up a prayer that the Lord would make me more like him. It was the desire of my heart.

My face felt flush, as tears welled up in my eyes, when I heard the lines, "You can talk about serving because you were a servant. You can talk about giving because you sacrificed." Next to the image of Jesus my attempts at service and giving paled greatly. Whatever I had done for God could hardly be referred to as a sacrifice.

Tears spilled from my eyes as the Holy Spirit showed me the truth about my life. I could be doing so much more than I was. I heard his call through the rich, nourishing sounds of the music.

Somehow I sang out loud with the song, "Serve through me. Give through me. Love through me. Live through me."

As if in response, I heard, "I wanna believe, but only you can change me."

I prayed, "Lord, change me. I want to be more like you. I'm sorry. I want you to live through me. Have your way with my life."

This intense release of emotions gave way to a sense of peace. A spirit of hope replaced the spirit of dread I had about returning home.

Only in hindsight, could I see this as the place of my rebirth, the time all things would become new. I spent the next seven hours of my drive home praising God. As I drove down the interstate, I prayed, making joyful noises, and thanking God for his grace and mercy. I wondered if anyone else on the road noticed the miraculous hand of God at work that day.

Over the next couple of weeks, God continued to speak to me about living what I believe. He was firm, but tender. He was patient, but relentless. Like Jacob in the book of Genesis, I wrestled with God to receive my blessing.

God let me know it was not his desire for me to divorce my husband. I knew what I wanted, but I also lacked the vision to comprehend how God was going to deliver. The Lord poured out his unconditional love on me. He showed me that he had forgiven me for my sins, though they had grieved him greatly.

God was faithful to provide sound counsel in the coming months, while he also began to work on softening my husband's cold and hardened heart.

I wish I could report this was the beginning of the end of the suffering I felt, but the flesh puts up a struggle. I can sympathize with the Apostle Paul's frustration, "Why do we do the things we do not want to do and not do the things we want to do?"

My husband and I finally found reconciliation. Today, we are blessed beyond measure to have our family together, with Christ at the center. We are learning to surrender ourselves daily to God. We can be free to experience his purpose for our lives. The truth is, God's ways are better than our ways and his plans far exceed anything we dare hope for or can even imagine.

"Lord, make me more like you so you can live on through this one. Loving you will bring me to live what I believe...Live what I believe."

I fell completely in love with Jesus, as I understood more about what he had done for me through this song. My life changed completely during that drive home. I felt like I was on a journey, listening to Anne MacCallum's CD and traveling with God. I have felt God's presence almost every day since.

SHELBY ROUNTREE

Shelby and her husband have two sons. Shelby serves as a volunteer in her church, her children's schools, and in her community. Shelby believes that books and music are two of God's greatest gifts to her, outside of her family.

HOLY IS THE LORD

// **PERFORMED BY ANDREW PETERSON** //

Wake up, Little Isaac
Rub your tired eyes
Go and kiss your momma
We'll be gone a little while
Come and walk beside me
Come and hold your Papa's hand
I go to make an altar
And to offer up my lamb

I waited on the Lord
And in a waking dream he came
Riding on the wind
Across the sand he spoke my name
And here I am, I whispered
And I waited in the dark
And the answer was a word
That came down hard upon my heart

Holy is the Lord, Holy is the Lord
And the Lord I will obey
Lord, help me, I don't know the way

So take me to the mountain
I will follow where you lead
And there I'll lay the body
Of the boy you gave to me
And even though you take him
Still I ever will obey
Make of this mountain
Please make another way

Holy is the Lord, Holy is the Lord
And the Lord I will obey
Lord, help me, I don't know the way

/// LETTING GO ///

BY STEVE NARROW

I knelt by my nineteen-year-old son's bed. I cried out from a depth of my spirit I had never felt before. I could only weep in prayer, trusting that God understood the groans and sighs of my soul, even though I couldn't utter the words.

As I felt the covers of his bed beneath me, I longed for the days of old. Timothy was young enough to be under my protective care and listen to my direction. I grieved for what might happen to him and my inability to reach him.

My son was practically homeless, yet refused to accept any help or advice. He had just finished his first year of college and had taken a summer job. The real world was waiting for him. I could only cringe when I imagined what his future held.

Divorce, attention deficit disorder, and other factors had been a part of his life. Timothy had been living with his mother, but their relationship was deteriorating. He was not able to respect the rules and guidelines that she had set down for him. His mother finally asked him to leave.

Timothy had always had a hard time yielding to even the good advice of others. He avoided discussions about his finances. He was spending impulsively and had little to show for his efforts. He tried to keep his business hidden from his family.

He was without a place to live, but unwilling to accept the help of others. I felt like I had lost any hope of reaching him.

Timothy insisted he would stay in the city instead of coming to live with me. He didn't want to give up the new job he had secured. His view of reality was quite distorted. He couldn't possibly comprehend how expensive it was to live and how little his paychecks would cover.

In my wildest imagination, I could not envision him being able to pay his rent or the utilities on time. In my flesh, I could only see him being evicted and being too ashamed to ask for help, essentially becoming homeless.

Days passed. I grew more frantic with each passing moment. My thoughts were consumed by my son—a man in body, yet lacking the adult experience or financial stability to make it on his own. I oftentimes prayed and turned him over to God, only to let my flesh take over again. Worry consumed me.

The very next morning, during my commute to work, the Andrew Peterson CD in my player rolled around to his song, "Holy is the Lord." I had heard this song many times. Each time I heard it, different images came to my mind. The words "as a sword upon my heart" pierced me deeply. The phrase confirmed the necessity of leaving things in God's hands.

The song talked about how Abraham was told to offer up his only son, Isaac. I could vividly see Abraham taking the hand of his child. He explained that they would be going on a long walk up the mountain. Isaac didn't understand what was in store for him. Abraham cried as they walked along the dusty and dry road.

"Why are you crying, papa?" I could hear Isaac ask. Abraham answered with a squeeze of the boy's hand. He was unable to speak. Abraham cried out from his heart, however, "Father, please, please make another way! Abraham never spoke those words aloud.

Abraham and Isaac reached the site and together, they began to build an altar of stone. Then, at once, the silence was broken.

"Isaac, come up here."

Abraham couldn't fathom how those words came from his mouth. As Abraham began to tie his son to the stones, innocent Isaac asks about the proceedings. Abraham had reached the place in his soul where he totally released his greatest treasure, his son born of a barren old wife, to God. How was he rewarded for such a yielding? God spoke and stopped the sacrifice of Isaac, replacing him with a ram.

After listening to the song, I realized I needed to trust that God had a loving plan for my son, as well. I knew that God had the perfect answer to this dilemma. I knew God didn't need my input while formulating his plan.

Timothy decided to move in with his friend's family. He finally realized the reality of trying to make it on his own in the city. Despite my fears and doubts, Timothy got back on his feet and is now growing in the Lord.

When I let go, it was as if I invited God to do his will in my son's life. Many times, our desires for the best will interfere with God's plan for the perfect.

STEVE NARROW

Steve is a retired probation officer. Steve runs a Drug Court program that targets specific criminal offenders and provides them with intensive treatment and supervision.

MANSION OVER THE HILLTOP

// WRITTEN BY IRA STANPHILL //

I'm satisfied with just a cottage below
A little silver and a little gold
But in that city where the ransomed will shine
I want a gold one that's silver lined

I've got a mansion just over the hilltop
In that bright land where we'll never grow old
And some day yonder we will never more wander
But walk on streets that are purest gold

Don't think me poor or deserted or lonely
I'm not discouraged I'm heaven bound
I'm but a pilgrim in search of the city
I want a mansion, a harp and a crown

I've got a mansion just over the hilltop
In that bright land where we'll never grow old
And some day yonder we will never more wander
But walk on streets that are purest gold

/// THE PERFECT CARD ///

BY SUE ANN RAY-WAGLE

I desperately searched through the sympathy cards, looking for the one that would best express my heart. I still couldn't believe my best friend's father was gone. In many ways, I thought of Jack Reitz as my own father.

I wished I could have been there for his funeral. I would have liked to pay my final respects. But I lived several states away. I knew it wasn't possible. A card was my only opportunity to express my condolences.

None of the cards seemed to say the right thing. I questioned if I would ever find the perfect message. I finally picked up a card and glanced at the words printed across the front. I fought tears. The words to the song "Mansion Over the Hilltop" brought back sweet memories.

Growing up in a dysfunctional home, I was taken under the wing of my best friend's parents. They had a strong Christian home. Her parents had been missionaries in Africa when she was young. Their home was filled with fascinating mementos of their time there. Their home reflected their strong faith and loving family life. I spent many happy hours as part of their family. The memories will be with me forever.

Some of my favorite memories were the times my friend and I rode in the car with her father. We sang hymns that I was familiar with, as we drove along. We attended a small Methodist church. During the summer we had an annual "hymn sing." We spent every night for one week in song services. During each service, the congregation chose some of their favorite hymns. Even as a young child, I enjoyed this event dearly.

"Mansion Over the Hilltop" was my favorite song. It made me think of a wonderful home where my beloved father waited with God for me. It was also my first introduction to harmony. My friend's father had a beautiful voice. Ruth sang along with him. I joined in on the melody.

I asked to sing that song over and over again. Sometimes we all sang it as many as four times during the short ride home! Those warm moments helped me make it through the cold ones that I faced after I returned home.

The memories washed over me as I read the words to that familiar song printed across the card. I knew the Holy Spirit had a hand in helping me find this sympathy card. It perfectly expressed the message I wanted to share with his family.

Today, I enjoy my roles as teacher and mother. I always try to keep in mind how much we can touch a child's life by the things we do and say. In my free time I sing in a trio. Music reminds me of the times we sang while riding in my Ruth's family car.

Jack Reitz may have never known what an influence he and his family had on my life. When I am feeling overwhelmed with the struggles this world presents I oftentimes find myself humming that hymn...

> I've got a mansion just over the hilltop,
> In that bright land where we'll never grow old.
> And someday yonder, we will never more wander,
> But walk on streets that are purest gold.

What a wonderful promise for a beautiful future!

ƧUE ANN RAY-WAGLE

Sue enjoys teaching sixth grade in the Omaha, Nebraska, school district. She spends as much time as possible with her teenage daughter and still loves to sing.

IMAGE OF

// PERFORMED BY MICHELLE TUMES //

I turned around today
Thought I saw you crying
Sad, defeated, so afraid
You're strong and beautiful
Oh, there's no denying
You're a child of light
Though shadows cloud your way

In your eyes I see love, I see laughter
I see hope for the dreams life has shattered
I can see in your eyes
It is Christ
It is love
You're the image of

In your face I see
Through the tears you're crying
Reflection of a risen Christ
So rise and feel the sun
Fly with wings of angels
Through the dark of the night
Feel your spirit burning bright

I'm so glad to see you smile
Compassionate and strong
Mirror image of his song
And I'm so glad to see you smile
It's Christ you're the image of

In your eyes I see love, I see laughter
I can see in your eyes it is Christ

/// IMAGE OF JESUS IN ME ///

BY VANESSA BRUCE INGOLD

I placed the phone on the receiver. A smile spread across my face, as I mentally replayed the conversation. My father had called to ask if he and his wife could come for a visit. The prospect caused me much excitement. This would be my Dad's first visit to California since my bicycle accident ten years earlier.

My father and I had a strained relationship for most of my life. Because of my parents' divorce, when I was six years old, I hadn't been close to him.

My mother oftentimes told me that it was my fault my father left. Her words pierced my heart throughout my childhood. I figured it was true since he never contacted me.

As my brother, sister, and I grew older, we also grew apart. After graduation from high school, I went to cosmetology school. When I was twenty, I moved to Long Beach, California to work as a hair stylist. There I met Cynthia, one of my coworkers.

Cynthia explained that she was a Christian. She invited me to church with her. I told her I would like to go. Yet, each Sunday something happened. The problem was sometimes with Cynthia's car, but more frequently the problems had more to do with my late Saturday night partying. The party life made it difficult for me to arise on Sunday morning.

One Thursday night in January, two weeks after my twenty-third birthday, I lay in bed crying. Suddenly, I felt like I had wasted my life. I was lonely and longed for family renewal.

I poured out my heart to God. "Please change me," I prayed. I asked God to somehow reunite and heal my family.

The next morning, even though I awoke to a cloudy and gloomy day, I took my usual bike ride to the gym. There was no bicycle lane on the road I traveled. I rode along with the traffic.

A guy who had parked his car in the parking lane opened his door. I swerved into the left turn lane toward oncoming traffic. Unfortunately, a Ford Ranger entered the lane and struck me head-on.

The doctors at the Long Beach Memorial Hospital emergency room were shocked to see tire tracks going across my chest at an angle. They began on the top left side of my body.

During a moment of lucidness, I asked if the hospital would call my best friend to let him know what happened.

When I opened my eyes from a medicated sleep, I saw my brother, sister, Mom and even my dad at my bedside. I discovered later that my friend had called them.

My father looked at me with concerned eyes. He didn't know what to say. I lay there with tears running down my face. The ventilator prevented me from speaking.

"This must be bad if Dad is here," I thought.

The mitral valve in my heart was ripped and the tricuspid valve was slightly damaged. Along with other short, irregular, and flat-shaped bones, every long bone in my body was fractured. My liver was severely lacerated, too.

Because of the severity of my injuries and the blood loss, the surgeons wanted to stall before replacing the mitral valve. But, when I experienced congestive heart failure they were quickened into surgery.

Before the operation, a priest was sent into my room to "read me my last rites." Doctors were not sure that I would survive.

I survived, however. After the surgery, I remained in ICU for three and a half months.

"Why me?" I asked God.

I felt as if he told me something important. "This will work together for good."

"But how?" I wondered.

After six months in the hospital, with a pig valve in my heart and a smile across my face, I hobbled out the rehab doors. Because gangrene set in, all ten of my toes had been amputated. I couldn't skip with my feet but my repaired heart skipped because of my friends and family's support.

My family's restored relationship made me happy. In addition, mine and my mom's relationship began taking a positive turnaround. My greatest pleasure, however, came by knowing that my dad truly cared about me. He asked if I would like to live with him and his wife. Although I was flattered, I declined. I loved California too much to leave.

Finally, a few months after I left the hospital, I started attending church with Cynthia. One night during a mid-week Bible study, I listened to the pastor as he read from Romans 8:28, "And we know that in all things God works for the good of those who love him, who have been called according to his purpose" (NIV).

Wow, God! You told me my accident would work together for good— and it did! Not only had the accident drawn my family together, but through the mishap, God's love began to soften my heart and helped me to forgive my mother.

Just when I would think I had completely forgiven her, however a bad memory would pop into my mind. The loss of being able to build a relationship with my father's family angered me. Yet, I learned to choose to forgive and love, regardless of my feelings. The more I realized that Christ had forgiven me for all my sins, and how he had paid for the sins that were committed against me, the more I experienced feelings of a sincerely forgiving heart.

Facing the opportunity to see my father again, I was reminded of God's peace. I praised God for healing my heart and for restoring my relationship with my entire family.

The next week, my dad and his wife treated my husband and me to a day at San Diego's Sea World. At the end of the day, Dad hugged me and said, " I am glad to see you so happy."

As my husband and I drove home, I played the Michelle Tumes's "Dream" CD. As the song "Image Of" played, I listened carefully to the words.

> In your face I see
> Through the tears you're crying
> Reflection of a risen Christ
> So rise and feel the sun
> Fly with wings of angels
> Through the dark of the night
> Feel your spirit burning bright

The song reminded me that I am God's child and also that he loves me. I was created in his image!

I pressed the repeat button. I was glad my relationship with my earthly father had been restored. It allowed me to see my Heavenly Father in an entirely new light. How terrible it would have been if I had a wrong image of my Heavenly Father!

Opening my heart to God as my Heavenly Father completed my healing process. He created me in his image, and through Jesus he had set me free. Therefore, I will forever walk as God's child, free to love and forgive, with a completely new heart.

VANEϟϟA BRUCE INGOLD

Vanessa was run over by a truck at age 23, resulting in twenty-six surgeries. Called a "walking miracle," she shares her experiences with interested groups. Vanessa and her husband Greg live in Southern California.

SUPERNATURAL

// PERFORMED BY DC TALK //

So many things to torment me
And as I stumble down this road
It takes a toll
These days and nights I turn to you
No human hand can pull me through
No cosmic force or magic brew
Will ever do

But I can see it coming
You're not so far away
'Cause I can feel your power surging
through the whole of me

Chorus

God is there and he is watching
He tells me all is well
God is there, there's no denying
It's supernatural
Supernatural
Beyond this physical terrain
There's an invisible domain
Where angels battle over souls
In vast array
But down on earth is where I am
No wings to fly, no place to stand
Here on my knees I am a stranger
In this land

I need an intervention
A touch of providence
It goes beyond my religion
To my very circumstance

Chorus

God is there and he is watching
The signs are everywhere
God is there, there's no denying
It's supernatural
Supernatural

Bridge

Six days a universe was made...
Supernatural
And from the dead a man was raised...
Supernatural
They say he walked across the waves...
Supernatural
And I'll believe it to my grave

/// TICKET TO HAPPINE// ///

BY VANESSA BRUCE INGOLD

I diligently fought depression during the winter of 1998. I had convinced myself I shouldn't be depressed since I had been a Christian for seven years. With a mechanically clenched smile, I had survived Thanksgiving, Christmas, and New Years.

Now, I had the post-holiday blues. "How are you?" was all one had to say for me to choke back my tears. I had not enjoyed the winter holidays for most of my life. Having come from a broken family, I didn't have many good memories of the season.

At the beginning of February, the love month, I was at home sick on a Saturday night. I had a sore throat and a sinus infection. After having had a total of twenty-three surgeries since an earlier bicycle accident, my immune system had not been as strong as it once had been. I became sick much easier than before.

As I sat on my sofa, I remembered God's many miracles of sustenance. Remembrance always sparked a ray of hope. I counted the blessings in my life. Then I turned the radio on to listen to my favorite Christian station.

"Welcome to Youth on Fire," the disk jockey shouted, as if he were on fire.

"That is the kind of attitude I need," I thought. I need to be on fire and to get out of this slump.

"Listen for our Touch-Tone dial, be the first to call, and win a pair of tickets to both performances of D.C Talk's 'Supernatural' concert tour in Southern California—San Diego Sports Arena and Universal Studio, Los Angeles."

DC Talk was my favorite group, so I wondered if that might be why God had allowed me to be at home. The two concerts were in opposite directions from my house. Both were only an hour away. "I'm close enough that I could to both concerts," I thought.

I dialed the station's number. I sat holding the phone, ready to press the redial button. I was feeling much brighter already.

As soon as I heard the Touch-Tone sound, I hit redial. My call was going through. The DJ announced I was the first caller. I couldn't believe it. Already, my blues started to dissipate. I praised God that I would get to see D.C. Talk in concert. I chalked the win up as another blessing on my list.

I invited my friend, Michelle, to go with me to the concert. After it ended, we stopped to talk to some friends standing near a set of double doors. The swinging doors opened. A woman walked out with her daughter. The child was holding tightly to her mother's hand and yawning. I glanced at the paper in her hands. I had to seize the opportunity.

"Is that a backstage pass?" I asked.

"Yes it is. It is my daughter's," the woman explained. "But she is only nine, and she's ready to go home."

She offered me the pass. My friend insisted that I go ahead without her. I walked in and saw a set up of snacks, bottled water, and soft drinks. A little farther, the three band members were dispersed. Small groups of people were gathered around each one.

I had fun talking to all three D.C. Talk members. Going backstage had made the concert even more exciting.

My blues began to disappear as the lyrics of DC Talk's songs ministered to my heart. Christian music was lifting me from my slump.

The next week, I went to the second concert with my friend, Christina. We got to the stadium about thirty minutes early. We sat down in our seats, which were only about ten rows away from the stage. I began talking with a guy sitting beside me. He told me he sang backup for one of D.C. Talk's songs on their Supernatural CD.

"You wouldn't happen to have any backstage passes would you?" I inquired.

He dug into his pocket. "Yeah, I do, here you go."

Both Christina and I marveled at God's supernatural intervention.

Finally, after the two opening groups, with dimmed lights, and D.C. Talk on stage, the sound of "Supernatural" music began.

The drumming became more intense. As they sang, "I can feel your power surging through the whole of me," I couldn't stay seated!

"Yes, Lord," I told God while standing, "Just like this song says, I had been down a tough road, during my childhood, and then again after having my accident. But, I turned to you. And in my darkest night, you knew I needed your intervention. You blessed me with exactly what you knew would touch me and bring me out of my depression—my dream concert, with backstage passes, twice. You gave me a double blessing! There's no denying it. You are in my every circumstance."

Joining in with the crowd's cheer, I yelled out, clapping my hands and keeping time with my feet. What a wonderful way to praise you Lord!

After D.C. Talk's performance, I bought a CD. The band signed it backstage. They all remembered me from the prior concert.

When the concert was over, I spent the night at Christina's house. I kept waking her up, because I couldn't stop giggling. The joy of the Lord overwhelmed me. I was still charged up from all of the excitement. I couldn't sleep.

God's special way of nudging me away from the blues blessed me greatly. He put a melody in my heart. I discovered that his joyful tune is my real "ticket to happiness."

VANESSA BRUCE INGOLD

Vanessa was run over by a truck at age 23, resulting in twenty-six surgeries. Called a "walking miracle," she shares her experiences with interested groups. Vanessa and her husband Greg live in Southern California.

FIND A WAY

// **PERFORMED BY AMY GRANT** //

You tell me your friends are distant
You tell me your man's untrue
You tell me that you've been walked on
And how you feel abused

So you stand here an angry young woman
Taking all the pain to heart
I hear you saying you want to see
  changes
But you don't know how to start

Chorus:
Love will find a way (How do you know)
Love will find a way (How can you see)
I know it's hard to see the past and still
  believe
Love is gonna find a way
I know that
Love will find a way (A way to go)
Love can make a way (Only love can
  know)
Leave behind the doubt
Love's the only out
Love will surely find a way

I know this life is a strange thing
I can't answer all the why's
Tragedy always finds me
And I'm taken again by surprise

I could stand here an angry young
  woman
Taking all the pain to heart
But I know that love can bring changes
And so we've got to move on"

Chorus

/// LOVE WILL FIND A WAY ///

BY DOUG VAN PELT

One day, during the summer of 1985, a song helped me through a really tough and dark time.

My story is a "prodigal son" story. I came to faith in Christ when I was 11 years old. The transformation of my conversion was real. It bore much fruit.

I fell in love with Jesus and yearned to know more about him. I highlighted my Living Bible like crazy. I was beginning to learn about worship and prayer. I also had the privilege of leading two of my best friends to Christ.

For some reason, this very real relationship only lasted about six months, however. The next nine years was a prodigal journey that started out with my own selfish living. The fruit it bore in later years was of a wanton and reckless lifestyle.

Nine years later, I was staying at my parents' home during the summer between my sophomore and junior years at college. One of my friends who I had met a summer or two before was hanging out with me.

Greg had "come back to the Lord" while I was away at school. He shared things with me about Jesus that I already knew and respected. He also shared some things that really intrigued me. The passage in 1 Peter 3:19 was one of those things. It says that Jesus preached to the "spirits in prison" after the crucifixion.

Greg had wept over the condition of my soul. He prayed and fasted for me. Through a series of events and the Lord's drawing me unto himself, my friend Greg had the privilege of leading me back to the Lord.

Two years later, Greg became my roommate at the home I rented in Austin, Texas. When it came to cleanliness and such, our habits differed. I grew tired of being his roommate. One night, I decided to have a talk with him. When he returned home from work, I announced, "Greg, I love you and I would fight for our friendship, but I am sick of being your roommate."

I'm not sure if he heard the preamble about loving him. But after he heard the "I'm sick of being your roommate," part he muttered something about the Hell that the preacher was talking about on the television. He marched into his room and slammed the door behind him. He threw open the window. The next thing I knew, he was throwing his possessions out on the lawn. He moved out that night.

This wasn't what I expected. I had truly offended my dear friend. Not only was he my friend, but also he'd had a part in leading me back to Jesus, making him even a more special friend. He found another place to stay. I was devastated. It hurt to know that I had ruined our friendship.

A song that played a great deal on the radio that summer, really spoke to me. It was called "Find A Way." The chorus promised that, "love will find a way."

I clung to that chorus like a promise from God. Even though I am normally a tough, macho guy, I still had my feelings hurt and I missed my friend.

I left notes of apologies on his windshield. The song really helped me get through that time. I trusted that God would see us through and that our friendship would be restored.

Sure enough, after a few more weeks Greg and I started talking to each other again. We were able to repair a great deal of the hurt that had come between us.

As the song says, "I know it's hard to see the past and still believe... Love will surely find a way..."

I cannot adequately describe the profound impact that song had on me that summer. That song helped me get through a tough time.

This reinforces my belief that the greatest or most used gift that contemporary Christian music offers is not evangelism (reaching the unbeliever), but pastoral (edifying the believer). Many people can look back over a particular time in their lives and remember how a song helped them sail through a rough time. I can certainly relate.

DOUG VAN PELT

Doug is the founder and editor of *HM*, a twenty-year-old Christian hard music magazine that covers the wide span of hard music including hardcore, metal, emo, rock, alternative, punk, ska and industrial. He has served as columnist for *CCM Magazine* and *Guitar World Magazine*. Doug lives in Austin, Texas.

I BURIED MY HEART AT BENDED KNEE

// WRITTEN BY MICHAEL ROE AND BRUCE SPENCER //

So long ago I drew a line
For myself in the sand
Time after time I moved that line when I
  crossed it again and again
Here we are back at the same old place
Down on the ground on my knees
But I'm still staring you right in the face

I know that I've been afraid
And I'm getting jaded more and more
  every day
I don't really care what anybody says
I ain't gettin' closer while I'm running
  away
How many times on a raging sea
If you see me going down, you gonna
  rescue me?
If I turn back to you on bended knee will
  you unlock my cage?
Will you set me free?
Set me free...

I've got a debt that I carry around
Carry around like a weight
It don't relieve me to know
That it's already paid
I've been a long, long way from my home
I went the wrong way
Now it seems I'm bound and determined
  to roam
Roam on babe

How many times in the burning heat,
If I go down in flames will you rescue
  me?
If I turn back to you on bended knee will
  you unlock my cage?
Will you set me free?
Set me free..."

/// BOUND TO FAIL GOD ///

BY BRET CHRISMER

I am originally from the St. Louis Metro area. For twenty years I have resided in Springfield, Missouri. I am a member of Park Crest Assembly. I grew up in church and around a great heritage of faith. I came to Springfield to attend college. While here, I fell in love, got married, and made this city my home.

Even though I have been a Christian for many years, there are times when I struggle with some of the things Christians come up against.

Satan sometimes tempts me to become complacent. At other times I wander away from the things that I know are right. The songs that hits me the hardest are the ones which deal with life issues and the ones that focus on repentance, forgiveness, thankfulness, and the amazement that God has great compassion for me.

I have been into music all of my life. I have a wide appreciation of styles. I would be hard pressed to have to choose a style of music that is my favorite. I guess you could say I like the ABC's of music—From Alternative Rock to Bluegrass, Black Gospel, Country, Classic Rock, Folk, Gospel, and Hymns, and all the way through to Zydeco.

My favorite artists or performers tend to be those whom are singer/songwriters. Something special happens when a singer sings the words, which come out of his or her own personal experience. They touch on emotions that someone who is merely covering a song cannot express.

One particular singer/songwriter, Michael Roe has greatly influenced my life over the years. He has dealt with life, "warts and all." Roe is the lead singer for The 77's. He is a member of the band "The Lost Dogs," as well as a solo artist.

There has been a variety of songs, which grabbed my attention and hit me right where I live. It is difficult to pick one particular song, out of the

886 tracks that I have in my library of songs that Roe has performed.

There is one song that I have lived out several times, however. It deals with the understanding that in life we are bound to fail God, yet God in his goodness will reach down and through his love, rescue us. It reminds me that even in my most miserable failures, God still loves me and will forgive me if I will receive his forgiveness. The song "I Buried My Heart at Bended Knee" is an example of that reminder.

Two years ago, I attended a church sponsored men's retreat. I went with a twenty-year chip on my shoulder. I had bad attitude toward the speaker, Reverend Oscar Symmes*.

He had no idea that I had been holding this grudge against him. He didn't even know me. I was angry at this man because of a sermon tape that a friend of mine brought back from church camp. Reverend Symmes spoke of the evils of "Rock Music." At the time, my friend's mom was on a crusade to clean up the radio listening habits of the youth in the church. I became angry with the evangelist! This affected me deeply. I did everything I could to avoid any church-related event where Reverend Symmes would be preaching.

Suddenly, I was at this men's retreat and he was the speaker. I sat with my arms crossed and my attention elsewhere when the service began. As Reverend Symmes preached, the Holy Spirit began working on me. He convicted of the rotten attitude that I had toward this man. That night, as I was lying in my bed, I listened to Michael Roe's album, "The Boat Ashore." When the song "Buried My Heart at Bended Knee" played, it gave me a different perspective. The moment I heard the words in that song, God began to change my thoughts.

Sometimes, I tend to try to take control of my own life instead of letting God have total control of it. At that point, he was ready to take control back. In "Bended Knee," the 'line I had drawn in the sand' haunted me for not dealing with my attitude about this preacher. I spent time that night burying my heart. As I lay there in my bunk, I felt God telling me that I had to ask forgiveness for the attitude I had toward this man.

The next day, as soon as I could find Reverend Symmes, I went to him and asked for his forgiveness. His reaction was one of total surprise. He was very gracious, however and told me I was forgiven. He thanked me for coming and talking with him. God "unlocked my cage" and took the weight of that grudge off my shoulders.

This is only one of the many examples of where I have allowed myself to become jaded in my Christian walk. It is not always about having a life-changing conversion such as Paul's.

My own conversion experience occurred when I was three years old. During my Christian walk, I have faced temptations that have tried to pull me away from my relationship with Christ. The most harmful temptations are the subtle ones that try to divert our focus from a pursuit of Godliness to the selfish things of life. The song, "I Buried My Heart at Bended Knee" helped me to regain my focus and continue to help me put Christ first in my thoughts and actions.

The words to this song are so very real to me. When Mike Roe sings the words, it reminds me of how, at times, we all struggle. Roe's life and his songs let me know that he is a Christian who calls on God to help him. Through this song he has encouraged me to do the same.

* Name used is in no way related to the real person.

BRET CHRISMER

Bret is a husband and the father of two lovely daughters. He and his family reside in Springfield, Missouri. Bret is actively involved with men's ministries, children's ministries, and his church's Missions Action Team.

HOME WHERE I BELONG

// PERFORMED BY CHRISTIAN EDITION //

They say that heaven's pretty
And livin' here is too
But if they said that I would
Have to choose between the two
I'd go home, goin' home
Where I belong

Sometimes when I'm dreamin'
It comes as no surprise
That if you'll look and see
The homesick feelin' in my eyes
I'm goin' home, I'm goin' home
Where I belong

While I'm here I'll serve him gladly
And sing him all these songs
I'm here, but not for long
When I'm feelin' lonely
And when I'm feelin' blue
It's such a joy to know that
I am only passin' through
I'm headed home, I'm goin' home
Where I belong

One day I'll be sleeping
When death knocks on my door
And I'll awake to find that
I'm not homesick any more
'Cause I'll be home, I'll be home
Where I belong"

/// CORNERSTONE ///

BY SANDY JAY

In the mid 1970s, my husband, Lewis, and I discovered Christian music festivals. At the time, we had four daughters, ranging in age from age eight to fourteen. We took the family to the Jesus '75 festival in Pennsylvania. We attended Creation Festival '83 in Pennsylvania where Steve Taylor played his first festival and introduced his debut album "I Want to Be a Clone."

At that same festival, I heard Mylon LeFevre share his testimony. I also heard Russ Taff perform. These three artists really made an impact on me.

Upon returning home from Creation Festival in 1983, I heard about a new Christian music festival called Cornerstone. It would be held near Chicago the next summer. My two young daughters and I attended the first Cornerstone Festival. What I experienced at Cornerstone changed my way of thinking more than anything ever had.

Growing up, I had diverse experiences with music. My earliest musical recollections are of the Dixieland music my father adored, as well as boogie-woogie music and jazz. While visiting with relatives in Kentucky at the age of eleven, I learned to love bluegrass and country music.

The following summer I attended a camp meeting where I accepted Christ. Even though the message at those camp meetings was delivered with the "hellfire and brimstone" approach, I knew even at the young age of 12 that I wanted to live my life for God. I committed my life to him at one of those camp meetings.

For many years, I did not listen to secular music because I had been told that it was "of the devil." As a teenager, I enjoyed listening to Southern Gospel quartet music as I read my Bible. I loved music so much that I purchased many records. If I wasn't listening to gospel music on the radio from radio station WLAC in Nashville, Tennessee, I was playing it on the record player.

My future husband, Lewis, and I met the year I turned seventeen. We both shared the same love of music. Along with his parents, Lewis and I attended gospel music events. After we were married, we continued to participate in all-night sings until we had our first child.

Eventually, our musical taste expanded. In the late 1960s, we discovered contemporary Christian music and artists like Andrae Crouch, Larry Norman, and The Bill Gaither Trio. We spent our time either attending concerts or purchasing records and listening to them on our stereo equipment.

As the Jesus Music era burst upon the scene in the late 1960s and very early 70s, we were really happy about this new kind of music called "contemporary Christian music." The decade of the 1970s was one where we were totally immersed in music, whether it was singing, attending concerts, or listening to the songs on our record player.

However, what we experienced at Cornerstone in the early 1980s was different than anything I had ever experienced before. There was so much love and acceptance expressed there. And because I sometimes felt lonely as a child, this was an event that helped me realize that everyone is truly loved and accepted by God. Everyone worshipped and praised God together.

At first glance, I noticed some strange looking people there. We saw tattooed people with all kinds of piercing and unconventional hairstyles. What stood out, however was the love and acceptance we felt there. In spite of individual differences, everyone came together as the body of Christ.

I was also exposed to and enjoyed all kinds of music, which I had never heard before. What fun it was to learn about all the different ways people can express their love for God. The thing that has always impressed me most about the Cornerstone festival is that the bands genuinely have a desire to spread the gospel, both by singing their songs and by preaching between songs.

At Cornerstone, everyone was accepted. I experienced a new understanding of Christian love. This love freed me from a lifetime of judging outward appearances. I began studying the Word of God more and learned a great deal about freedom in Christ. As a result, my judgmental attitude ebbed away, little by little.

Every person has the desire to be accepted. We all want to belong. Through experiences like Cornerstone, I have learned that God accepts and loves me just as I am.

My favorite song and the one that holds the most meaning for me is "Home Where I Belong" by Pat Terry. For the majority of my life, I felt like a misfit here on earth. I felt like someone who doesn't belong. "Home Where I Belong" is one song that expresses my heart perfectly. It lets me know that the feeling is not unique to me. There are many other songs which have ministered to me over the years, as well. But this one stands alone. It has comforted me over and over again. The song is very simple, but also sincere and real.

Today, it is sometimes difficult to decide which kind of music to play. We have a lot of good Christian music to choose from in our music library. I realize that God has used many different styles of music to bring me closer to him and to show me where I belong.

SANDY JAY

Sandy and her husband of forty-three years have four daughters and eight grandchildren. She works from home as a medical language specialist. Together with one of their daughters, they are also wildlife rehabbers, nursing orphaned and injured animals before releasing them back into the wild.

I NEED GOD

// **PERFORMED BY MICHAEL ROE** //

I need God in all the familiar places
That this lonely heart of mine embraces
Oh I need God
Well, I need God but I've wandered so far away
More and more each and every day
I go astray

Well, his open arms reach out to me
Longing and begging to set me free
Will I reach out and take them or turn
Away and forsake them?
No, no, no...

Well, I need God
But I wonder if he can still hear me, and if so,
Won't you please draw near to me
Oh, please, please God"

/// WINNING OVER LOSS ///

BY BRET CHRISMER

there have been so many times that I wandered away from God and followed my own direction. There have been many distractions in my life. Sometimes, I lose my focus and fail to follow God's leading. Although I know I need God, sometimes, I forget just how much I need him.

The large telecommunications company where I work has been struggling to increase its stock price since the stock market fell in 2001. They have been cutting costs everywhere, reorganizing the stock structure, and selling some of the debt-laden business segments. Unfortunately, the stock price has continued to decrease.

One day, I received a call from the corporate office in another city. I was notified that there would be a layoff, which would cause a job loss for one of the representatives in Springfield, Missouri.

I somehow knew deep within my heart that I might be the one who would soon be without a job. Going on my own intuition, I began preparing my wife for what might come. I asked my friends, family, and church to pray that God would provide the right job for me and that he would reveal his plan to me in this situation.

On June 28, 2004, I received the dreaded call I had expected. I had sixty days to find a new job. I am not a Christian who only calls upon God during a time of crisis. But it sometimes takes a crisis to remind us that during times of struggle, we draw closer to God.

It had been over three months since I lost my job. Although I sent my resume to dozens of companies and had been to several interviews, no suitable job offer materialized. During this time, several people said things like "You're a smart guy with a great personality. You won't have any trouble finding a job." Yet here I am, still waiting on God to provide the right opportunity for me.

Those of you that have been down this road know the difficulties a job loss causes. Many times I left an interview feeling very confident that I would receive an offer. Then later I would receive the standard "you are a great candidate, but we hired someone else" rejection letter in the mailbox.

It would be easy to become discouraged by my situation. But I continue to hold on to the thought that "God's love is amazing!" Through this time of uncertainty, God has used my family and friends to strengthen my spirit and remind me to depend on God. Their prayers and God's subsequent responsive reassurance are what keeps my focus on his promises. God is the owner of all creation and of every possibility that exists. He promises to provide for us. I know that in God's time I will have the new job that he has chosen for me. I am waiting on him for that to happen.

Whenever my job search gets me down, I think of Michael Roe's song "I Need God." Roe is one of my favorite singers. He recorded the song on his 1995 solo album "Safe As Milk." This is a powerful song. It speaks to me every time I hear it. I can listen to it many times over. Sometimes I play it on the guitar and sing it to God as a confession of my dependence on him. "I Need God" is a song that has been in steady rotation at my house. I find comfort in the song. The lyrics acknowledge my human tendency to stray away from God. They reveal the character of God "longing and begging to set me free," as I acknowledge the fullness of God.

The idea of a need for God is a fundamental one. I sometimes find myself taking for granted the fact that I need God and that he is always there for me. I know God is an unfailing God Who has his arms stretched out to me when I need him.

BRET CHRISMER

Bret is a husband and the father of two lovely daughters. He and his family reside in Springfield, Missouri. Bret is actively involved with men's ministries, children's ministries, and his church's Missions Action Team.

CHANGE MY HEART OH GOD

// WRITTEN BY EDDIE ESPINOSA //

Change my heart oh God,
Make it ever true.
Change my heart oh God
May I be like you.
You are the potter
I am the clay,
Mold me and make me,
This is what I pray.

/// A CHANGE OF HEART ///

BY MARTHA POPE GORRIS

As a Navy wife for almost twenty years, I was no stranger to separations. My husband Fred was a surface warfare officer. That meant he served aboard ships, and ships that go to sea.

During the first year we were married, Fred was deployed to the western Pacific, with a planned liberty stop in Hong Kong. Several of the officers' wives planned to fly over for a reunion. For two months I planned special gifts to bring and bought new clothes, which helped me to get through the long days of waiting.

On the morning our flight was to depart, I was just about to leave the apartment when the telephone rang. It was the captain's wife. "Martha? Sit down. I have some bad news."

My heart sank. "What?" I knew my voice was high, thin and shaky.

"I just got word that a typhoon is approaching Hong Kong within several days. If it keeps coming, the ship won't be able to enter the Hong Kong harbor."

"Oh no." Tears of disappointment threatened, but determination filled me. "I don't care! I'm still going. I'll take my chances."

There was a slight pause. "If you're going, I am too. We can share a hotel room until they come."

Some wives stayed home, others went. We spent a couple of uncertain days keeping watch on the harbor from our hotel room. Finally, the captain's wife got a call from the port authority. The ship was coming into Hong Kong harbor! I felt a relief so deep, I hadn't realized how wound up I had been. I had missed my sweetheart so much.

Fred had numerous three-month and six-month long deployments overseas. In preparation for these deployments, the ship and crew often had to leave port on Monday through Friday for training exercises. So, even before they left for their tour, they had already been gone for weeks. On the day of departure, we would wave until the ship was out of sight. After that, there was no communication, sometimes for weeks at a time.

A Navy wife has to be mom and dad while her spouse is away. We are on duty twenty-four hours a day, seven days a week with our children. We hold the sole responsibility of diapering, doctoring, and carpooling. We face the very difficult problems alone such as digging out of a flooded house or discovering and dealing with a house break in.

Because of the hardships of being a military wife, it is not a lifestyle many women would choose for themselves. The choice was a simple one for me, however. I fell in love with a military man. We met while Fred was attending the United States Naval Academy. We dated for three years and married a few days after his graduation and commissioning. I knew without a doubt that Fred was the one with whom I wanted to spend my life with. Being a young idealist, I didn't think twice about the hectic lifestyle.

Over time, second thoughts did creep into my mind. Gradually, I learned how to cope with all the separations and the lack of communication. When the blues began to bog me down, survival mode kicked in. I stayed busy with church, called friends, or volunteered for another committee at school.

We had been married about twenty years when orders came for Pentagon duty in Washington, DC. We bought a house in northern Virginia, settled into shore duty with gusto, and the family thoroughly enjoyed having Dad around. It was a sweet taste of civilian life complete with barbeques and football games. We had the ability to plan events a couple of months in advance. What a treat!

Finally, the day came for which we had all been hoping and praying— the coveted orders for a command at sea assignment! These orders were what Fred had spent his entire career working towards— Commanding Officer of a Navy destroyer. Making matters better, we would be moving back to San Diego, our favorite homeport.

The only downer in the equation was that Fred had to attend nine months of Commanding Officer School in Newport, Rhode Island before taking command of the ship. Our daughters were in high school and junior high. They had already left their friends in California the previous year. They had just become acclimated to the changes of life in Virginia and changes in schools and friends. Rather than uproot them again, we decided I would stay in the Washington area with the girls while my husband went to Newport alone.

When Fred left for Newport, I kissed him good-bye. I tried to be cheerful, struggling to fight off the all too familiar loneliness. "But God, this isn't what marriage is all about, is it?" I prayed. "I wish we could be together as a family!" I knew God would see us through this separation, but a heaviness of heart haunted me while I tried to exercise my usual coping skills. The longer we were married, the harder it was to say good-bye.

Every few weeks, my husband made the nine-hour drive to D. C. then back again two days later. For a change, I suggested meeting him halfway for a weekend. The girls were excited to stay with friends. Fred and I met in Pennsylvania on a Friday evening.

Those two days were a wonderful blend of uninterrupted conversations and exchanged details of everyday life. Somehow, those conversations were overlooked in phone calls. We lingered over meals. For two luxurious mornings, we slept in. We took a long leisurely walk through the autumn leaves and had a romantic dinner out. It was a mini second honeymoon.

All too soon, it was time to say good-bye again. I dreaded it. With each passing minute, a dark cloud loomed closer. I fought back tears, as I packed my bag. I wanted to be cheerful and upbeat, but the separations seemed to be getting harder, not easier with the passage of time. Somehow, I knew thinking happy thoughts and volunteering for another committee wouldn't do it this time.

My husband helped me load my car. As I drove away, I watched him in the rear view mirror. I thought about how we always seemed to be going in opposite directions. "Is this what our married life will always be like, Lord?" I whispered.

It started to rain, adding to my gloomy feeling. With each click of the windshield wipers, my thoughts seemed to get darker and more discordant. How many times had we said good-bye over the course of our lives? There had been so many separations. We had lived apart so much of the time. All those daily details that make a life special had been lost. The summer evenings listening to the kids playing ball outside were lost. It seemed like we were doomed to be apart.

Dismal tears washed over my heart. As I sobbed harder, the unhappy thoughts tumbled one over the other. Finally, I cried out, "Lord, please help me! I feel so lonely."

Almost immediately, a crisp, clear thought crossed my mind. Turn on the praise tape.

Grumbling, I pushed the tape into the cassette player. I let the familiar songs fill the car with the joy I didn't feel. Soon, the peppy music captured me. I started humming. Then I sang the words. It wasn't until I heard "Change my heart, oh God," that I realized I felt differently. "Change my heart, oh God, make it ever true, change my heart, oh God, make me more like you." With those simple but heartfelt words, I felt joy. Gone was the dark blanket of depression. I don't know how long I praised and worshiped God that night. What I do know is that I stopped thinking about all we had missed during our military life. Instead, as I sang along, my heart rose up with gratitude to God. With gratefulness, I thanked him for a wonderful weekend away, for a time of refreshment and renewal with my husband. I thanked him for happy children waiting at home for me. God answered my prayer by reminding me of the best survival skill of all—praise and worship lifted up to his glory. He alone could change my heart.

MARTHA POPE GORRIS

Martha is an active writer whose work has appeared in many publications. She has been married for thirty-two years to a former career naval officer, has two grown daughters, and resides in San Diego.

LET US RUN

// **WRITTEN BY MARTY GOETZ** //

Chorus
Let us run run run the race with endurance
Laying aside every weight
Casting aside every sin
Let us run run fixing our eyes on the Son
Looking to him finishing what we've begun
Let us run

Can you see how we are surrounded
By so great a cloud of witnesses
Those who paid the price
The supreme sacrifice
Those of whom this world was not worthy

And can you see now we are entrusted
With continuing what others started
They have passed the baton
Straight and fast till we've won
We will run for him who is holy

Bridge
Oh and yes there are some who have stumbled, fallen
God only knows I am one
Still I press toward the goal
For the Lord who's callin' me
He's gone before he's my reward
When I am done let us run.

/// STRESS UNDER CONTROL ///

BY MARLENE BAGNULL

I never understood my coworkers' response to my enthusiastic approach to looming deadlines. They thought I was strange! I figured that rising to the challenge and meeting it was the reason God had called us to work in an editorial office where deadlines were a given. The three new deadlines that marched on the heels of each deadline we met didn't faze me. I was young and filled with energy to run whatever race was set before me.

I remember the day the pressure became too much for my boss. After a stern warning from the head of production that she could not keep missing deadlines, she put her head down on her desk and wept. Dismayed, I determined not to let it happen again. The color-coded flowchart of upcoming deadlines that I posted on a large bulletin board in her office would have impressed anybody.

Sadly, for my boss it only justified her "right" to be overwhelmed by her workload. So I worked harder and put in longer hours. I took work home. I would do whatever it took to meet the deadline.

Years later, running the race in the "real world" of changing diapers, doing laundry, preparing meals and keeping a path cleared through the pile of toys in the living room didn't seem quite as exciting. My children did not share my idea of having a clean and orderly house. My husband preferred sitting in front of the television to tackling my never-ending "honey-do" list.

I turned to church work to fill my need to accomplish something meaningful. It didn't take long for me to be in over my head. I raced to stay on top of things that needed to be done both at home and at church.

My children grew and became involved in numerous activities. Chauffeuring them to music lessons, sporting events, and scouts added to the already full days. But I told myself that it was good to stay busy. After all, busyness was the American way!

By the time I reached fifty, my youngest child was in college. My middle child was in medical school and my oldest was married. I had a growing ministry. I was writing, speaking, and directing a large Christian writers' conference. After half a century of running, it had become a way of life. I had a good life, most of the time.

Although it was no longer as easy to run from morning until night, I determined to continue the race. Deadlines, however, had become something I dreaded rather than welcomed. I could relate more to my former boss. I worried that I would crumple under the stress.

I was the director of two, three-day Christian writers' conferences. They consumed more and more of my time. "Conference details are like the tentacles of an octopus," one friend said. "You think you have them under control and another tentacle escapes." What also escaped me was sleep. There was no way to avoid late-night and sometimes all-night work hours. "Sleep is a waste of time," I said many times. Now I wonder how I could have said that.

"You need to take the time to come to Marty's concert," a friend said. She had noticed the stress I was under and knew I needed to take a break. "Please come," she urged.

It would have been all too easy to forget her invitation with the deadlines I needed to meet. Something she said, however, kept resonating in my heart. "He is a worshipper." And so, even though I really was too busy, I ended up squeezing into a packed church that Friday night.

"Adonai, Adonai, Adonenu. . . ." From the first words Marty Goetz sang, I was ushered into God's presence. The weight of the stress I had been carrying was replaced by God's peace that passes understanding.

Marty sang for well over an hour. When it came time for the benediction, I slipped out just long enough to purchase his CDs and a video. Then I pressed my way back into the sanctuary. I felt drawn to get as close as possible to this Messianic Jew who obviously knew Jesus Christ, whom he called Yeshua.

One song that Marty sang that night stood out in my mind for months to come. "Let us run, run, run the race with endurance," Marty sang. As I reflected on the words Marty had written, the race took on new meaning. Yes, I had "stumbled and fallen." It had been all too easy to get caught up in the goal of serving the Lord that I had squeezed him into a smaller and smaller corner of my busy days. I had been running on empty!

Like a deer that pants for the water brooks, my spirit was drawn back to the Lord. God encouraged me. He lifted me up as I confessed my failure to keep my eyes on him and to trust fully in him. I also asked forgiveness for my "poor me" attitude. Of course, the work of the ministry is demanding and oftentimes difficult.

Of course, there will always be times when people disappoint me and let me down. Many times, it would be easier to give up. But how could I have forgotten the first words the Lord had ever spoken to me. "I never promised it would be easy to follow me, but I have promised always to be with you."

I thought of the "cloud of witnesses." These are the people who have gone on before me, willing to pay the "supreme sacrifice." What is a heavy workload and an occasional sleepless night compared to the persecution that Christians have endured throughout the centuries and continue to endure today?

"Laying aside every weight, casting aside every sin... fixing [my] eyes on the Son" I continue to recommit myself to running the race God has set before me in his strength and for his glory.

MARLENE BAGNULL

Marlene has written, compiled, and edited numerous books. She directs the Colorado and Greater Philadelphia Christian Writers' Conferences.

TOO LATE

// **PERFORMED BY AMY GRANT** //

Chorus:
Well, it's too late for walking in the
  middle,
Too late to try.
Yes, it's too late for sitting in the
  balance,
No more middle line.

Oh, it's too late for walking on fences,
Time to choose your side.
Yes, it's too late for flirtin' with the
  darkness,
Make up your mind.

Oh, the time has come for making a
  decision,
And you say you've found the light.
But the talk is cheap when I see the way
  you're living,
Walking in the night.

Chorus
Oh, it's too late for thinking you can walk
  the middle line...
Better get wise.

You may think that you can live by your
  feelings,
Different every night.
But an emotional religion will crumble at
  our feet,
If we're made to stand and fight.
Well, it's too late for walking on fences,
Time to choose you side.
Yes, it's too late for flirtin' with the
  darkness,
Make up your mind.

Well, it's too late for thinking you can
  walk the middle line...
Better get wise.

Chorus
Oh, it's too late for walking on fences,
Time to choose your side.
Yes, it's too late for flirtin' with the
  darkness,
Please make up your mind.

Chorus
Oh, it's too late for walking on fences,
Time to choose your side.
Yes, it's too late for flirtin' with the
  darkness,
Please make up your mind."

/// THE CHOICE IS OURS ///

BY JULIE PIERCE

i heard this great song blast over the speakers as I skated across the rink. I think it was the first time I had ever heard a Christian song that sounded like rock music. I was in my early teens and had only heard the kind of Christian music that my parents played.

The song was Amy Grant's "Too Late" from her "Live in Concert: Volume II" album. I thought it was the coolest song I had ever heard. I bought the album soon after the skating party. I was inspired by the lyrics of "Too Late." The message it portrays is that we have to choose whether or not we are true believers in Christ and whether or not we are going to live like Christians.

Some of the words that caught my attention were "Too late for walkin' in the middle...too late for walkin' on fences...too late for sitting in the balance...time to choose your side." This song had quite an impact on my decision to be bold in my Christian witness around my friends at school.

I also enjoyed Petra's albums when I was a teenager! "Stand Up" had much the same effect on me as Amy Grant's "Too Late." I was inspired with the energy. I was greatly encouraged to do as the song said, "Take a stand for Jesus...Stand up...'til the whole world sees us!"

Those songs and many other contemporary Christian songs motivated me throughout my teen years. I felt reassured by them. I loved the sound of Christian rock music and was thrilled that I had discovered it.

I grew up as a pastor's daughter. I had been well fed spiritually. If I had only lived my parent's teachings or the lessons learned from my upbringing at church, however, I would have fallen flat on my face. I would not have done anything that would have made a difference in the lives of my friends.

As a teen in high school I had to make a decision. "Too Late" gave me the desire to find confidence in the fact that I was a believer in Christ. It permeated all of my activities from how I behaved whether or not I got the part in the school musical I wanted, to how I reacted when a boy I liked wanted me to be less than virtuous!

On the other hand, I could have been more veiled in my beliefs. I could have compromised on a few issues here and there to maintain a more comfortable existence during my high school days. I continue to have to make that same decision today. All believers do. "Too Late" was a shot in the arm that helped me realize I wanted to be bold.

I didn't intend to wind up working at a radio station but God brought my husband, Daryl, who was called into Christian radio, into my life and placed me at this station. Here, I am able to express my passion for the incredible good I believe music can do. I am able to see the results from my listener's testimonies on a continual basis.

To this day I continue to be moved by contemporary Christian music and still prefer the rock sound. I am encouraged by it. I think that without this type of music, there would be an enormous hole and great darkness in the world.

There is so much garbage being pumped to us on a daily basis, that I find listening to Christian music to be a "cleansing" experience. I am convinced that if all Christians would listen to contemporary Christian music on a regular basis, they would find themselves spiritually stronger. Their hearts would be lighter. And they would become more motivated as believers in a time when the pressure to be mediocre in our faith is stronger than ever.

I can already see the influence of Christian music on my children, especially my soon to be ten-year-old son. He recently told me that his favorite song is Michael W. Smith's version of "Above All." He said, "I love that last line, 'Like a rose trampled to the ground, you took the fall, and thought of me, above all.'" (He always holds that last line out quite dramatically.) And yes, I believe he knows what it means.

At his tender age that song is moving him, just like Amy Grant's song moved me many years ago. I pray that he and his sister grow up to be committed to Christ in every way. I believe with all of my heart that contemporary Christian music will play a part in their faith and Christian walk.

JULIE PIERCE

Julie and her husband live in Cincinnati where they work on the air at WAKW radio. They have two children.

MOMMA, I

// PERFORMED BY EDDIE HEDGES //

Momma, I want to cry
But I promised you that
I'd be strong on the day you'd go away
To be with God almighty oh
Momma, it's so hard to stand here
And tell myself I'll be alright
So Momma please send me the
   strength
Momma, I know that you
Will be singing with me everyday
And I will keep you with me
In my heart where you will always stay
Momma, since you're right there with
   God
Standing beside him in heaven's
   garden
Ask him with me to send me more
   strength

Momma, I know I'm gonna see you
   again
But I need more strength to carry on
   until then
So help me ask the Lord to give me
   more
'Til I see you again at heavens door
I want to cry but Momma, I
Promised I'd be strong and carry on

Momma, I'll remember you
For everything you were to me
And I'll live my life for God
That's the only way that I will be
Together with you once again
We'll praise the Lord and oh how we'll
   sing
Momma, please send me more strength

So blessed was I to be right by your side
When the Lord came to give you your
   new life
With no pain, no worry again
You'll rejoice everyday Momma
Oh I can't wait

Momma, I promised I'd be strong and
   carry on
Momma, help me to be strong and carry
   on

/// MY MOM'S STORY ///

BY MICHELLE AUFDENKAMPE

On February 1, 2004, my mother, Mickey, was diagnosed with ovarian cancer.

I walked into her hospital room. "I have cancer, and I am going to die," she announced. My Mom was like a rock. She raised ten kids without any complaint or regret.

"Not today!" I announced. Mom had never been afraid before this. I prayed over her and with her. I wanted to help ease her fears.

Through the five weeks of her illness, I sang to her, prayed with her, laughed with her, rubbed her feet, held her hand, and encouraged her to remain positive.

"What are you thinking about Mama?" I asked her sometimes when she looked around the room at night.

"Just everything in general, I guess," she replied.

She returned home from a traumatic visit to the hospital, just a week before her passing. I was with her. For the entire month that she was sick, Mom slept in the recliner. If she tried to lie down in her bed, she would lose her breath.

She was about 4'10" and weighed only 130 pounds. Mom was not heavy enough to keep the recliner in an open position, so I held it down with my knee. I played with her hair while she slept. When she awoke one day she wanted to get in her bed. Then she asked to see all of her children. I thought she might be ready to leave this world, so I called all of my brothers and sisters. I told them to come quickly.

We put Mom in bed and sang to her. She tried to participate but mostly she slept. My brother watched over her the entire night. He didn't want her to be alone if she passed away that night. We could not get her into Hospice care that night without sending her back to the hospital. As a family, we decided that putting her in the hospital was not an option. My father held her hand for hours.

Finally, we asked him to get in bed with her and hold her tightly. It was the last night they shared their bed.

Mom passed away on March 4, 2004, at 10:15 a.m. We were all in the room with her. It was both the sweetest and the most painful moment of my life. Music was playing in the room. We were praying over her and telling her how much we all loved her. I cannot express how hard losing my Mother was.

A short time passed by. I was blessed by Eddie Hedges when he sang at my church, Horizon Community Church. I got his CD that day. I played the CD in my car, as my Dad and I were riding to the cemetery. I heard just the beginning of "Momma, I."

At that moment, I could not bear to hear the song or to watch my Dad cry, so I turned it off. When I took my Dad home, I took another car ride just to hear the song. I had to pull over when I listened to the words. I sobbed like a baby.

It was as if Eddie had written the song just for me. He knew exactly what I was feeling. Later, I shared the song with my brothers and sisters. Through "Momma, I" we were able to connect. We better understood our feelings.

Holidays, including Mother's Day, our parents' wedding anniversary and her birthday were not far away. I was dreading them! I didn't want to face the holidays without my mother. I knew that all of the "firsts" without her would be so hard. On these occasions, I played the song and drove to the cemetery.

Whenever I think about my mother, I play the song and somehow it helps me to deal with the pain. Sometimes I miss her so much that I feel I cannot breathe. The song has led me through these dark times. It has also given me peace when I write in my journal. Eddie Hedges song "Momma, I" touches my heart in a way that cannot be explained in words.

After I heard the song, I emailed Eddie to thank him for his heart for the Lord. I wanted to tell him that his voice reached into my heart like a warm blanket. He emailed me back the very next day to tell me he would pray for me on Mother's Day!

I loved my Mother with all of my heart. I shared everything about my life with her. My greatest joy was being able to make her laugh. Her eyes sparkled. She was blessed with 58 years of marriage with my father, and ten children. We all miss our mother very much, but through "Momma, I" Eddie has given us comfort and eased the way!

MICHELLE AUFDENKAMPE

Michelle is the mother of a grown son and a young daughter. Michelle is a Realtor in Cincinnati.

HIS EYES

Sometimes his eyes were gentle
And filled with laughter,
And sometimes they cried;
Sometimes there was a fire
Of holy anger,
In Jesus eyes.
But the eyes that saw hope in the
    hopeless,
That saw through the fault to the need,
Are the same eyes that look down from
    heaven
Into the deepest part of you and me.

Chorus:
His eyes are always upon us;
His eyes never close in sleep.
And no matter where you go,
You will always be in his eyes, in his
    eyes.

Sometimes his voice comes calling
Like rolling thunder,
Or like driving rain;
And sometimes his voice is quiet,
And we start to wonder
If he knows our pain.
But he who spoke peace to the water
Cares more for our hearts than the
    waves,
And the voice that once said "You're
    forgiven,"
Still says "You're forgiven" today.

Sometimes I look above me when stars
    are shining
And I feel so small;
How could the God of heaven and all
    creation
Know I'm here at all.
But then in silence he whispers,
"My child, I created you too
And you're my most precious creation;
I even gave my Son for you."

Chorus

Sometimes his eyes were gentle, and
    filled with laughter

Words by Steven Curtis Chapman and James Isaac Elliott. © 1989 Sparrow Song (admin. by EMI Christian Music Publishing) / Careers—BMG Music Publishing / Greg Nelson Music / ASCAP. All rights reserved. Used by permission.

/// HIS EYES ARE UPON ME ///

BY DEWAYNE HAMBY

One morning when I stood in front of the mirror, instead of the usually normal thoughts such as "I've got to get a haircut," my thoughts carried a much harsher tone. "You're always going to be fat." "You should be ashamed to walk outside your front door, looking the way you do." "You're totally alone."

The memory of that morning stands out as one that was more than just an average bad day. I have memories of other days when things went wrong, such as misplacing my keys or running late, but this was much more of an emotional heaviness which weighed me down.

That mental assault was so direct and so outside of the ordinary that I knew it was a highly organized spiritual attack. I knew the insulting daggers came from someone who despised the very one in whose image I was created. This realization came as little comfort at the time, however. I was not in any condition to go to battle with the adversary. This was my weakest moment.

There have been days when I would get up on the wrong side of the bed. Mondays and, as much as I hate to admit it, Sundays frequently fall into that category. Perhaps it is the change of routine combined with locating the right outfit, matching socks, bad hair days and running late that put me in a bad mood. Normally, these days are also characterized by noble plans of better organization for the future. But the way I felt that morning, was more than just about having a bad day.

I realized that sometimes we put too much focus on ourselves, our appearance, or our circumstances. These things can weigh us down or bring about discouragement. This was one of those times when I needed to be reminded that God was watching out for me, loved me, and that he wanted only his best for my life.

I was a believer. In fact, my whole world was centered on Jesus. I was writing for a Christian magazine, surrounded by Christian friends and very involved in church. Yet, I felt that I was living in a spiritual limbo. I was facing another crossroad in my life, a point where I would have to decide if I would stay in the same job at the same location. I had been seeking God's direction, but felt my prayers were going unnoticed. Doors were not opening and I didn't feel even a hint of divine guidance.

Satan doesn't believe in fair fights. He chose an opportune time to wage this war. He knew that I had come home several times and crawled upon my couch, sobbing. He may have even been aware of the calls I had made, the resumes I had sent out, and possibly my visible frustration at a perceived absence of God's intervention in my life. Satan smelled my weakness and came in for the kill.

Without a reasonable defense, I took this baggage out the front door. I would once again go through the day plastering a smile on my face in a defiant refusal of help. "Whatever it took," I decided, "I would survive to feel God's presence again...one day."

When I turned the ignition in my car, a very familiar voice came through the speakers. The disc playing was Steven Curtis Chapman's Greatest Hits. I had spent the past few days driving around listening to "Lord Of The Dance" and "The Great Adventure," which were a couple of his more upbeat pop tunes. Every time a slower song began playing, I would skip it, partly to avoid the mellower mood I had been fighting.

At this moment, a ballad was playing. I had heard it many times before, but somehow it felt like it was truly the first time I had ever really listened. With my captive attention, these particular words reverberated in my spirit:

> How could the God of heaven and all creation
> Know I'm here at all.
> But then in silence he whispers,
> My child, I created you too
> And you're my most precious creation;
> I even gave my Son for you.

His eyes are always upon you;
His eyes never close in sleep.
And no matter where you go,
You will always be in his eyes, in his eyes.

It was almost an indescribable moment—when those words came rushing into my brain. In the midst of an all-out war on the very fiber of my emotions, I was suddenly reminded how loved and cherished I was by the only one whose opinion truly mattered! With all the subtlety of a catchy melody and cleverly worded lyrics, God had shouted from the rooftops of my soul an eternal truth, "Surely I am with you always, to the very end of the age" (Matthew 28:20, NIV).

Being involved in the Christian music industry for years, it was very easy to hear a song so often that I just didn't "hear" it anymore. That was the case with "His Eyes." God breathed truth back into that song for me, cueing it to the exact part of the song he wanted me to hear. And yes, it did change my life.

Whenever anyone asks me if God has ever spoken to me, I share that without a doubt he arranged my song selection that day. God could have done any number of things to get my attention, to let me know he was fighting my battle for me, but he used a familiar voice and a guitar.

Thank God for musicians who continue to draw near to him and remind people like me how great, marvelous and wondrous God's love really is.

For believers, musicians serve as incredible encouragement. For "pre-Christians" they're a four-minute glimpse into eternal life and his abundant grace. I will hear thousands of songs before I die. I pray that the Lord will keep my heart pliable and always ready to be changed again.

DEWAYNE HAMBY

DeWayne currently lives in Cleveland, Tennessee, where he currently serves as writer and music section editor for *Christian Retailing* magazine.

GO ASK

// **PERFORMED BY THE BILL GAITHER TRIO** //

Don't ask me to explain for you how one could start again;
How hardened hearts could soften like a child.
Don't ask me how to reason out the mysteries of life,
Or how to face its problems with a smile.

Go ask the man who's found the way through tangled roads back home to stay, when
all communications were destroyed.
Go ask the child who's walking now, who once was crippled then somehow her useless
legs were made to jump for joy.
Go ask the one whose burned out mind has been restored, I think you'll find the
questions not important as before.
Don't ask me if he's good or bad; I only know the guilt I had is gone, and I can't tell
you anymore.

Don't ask me how to prove to you why I know God is there,
And how I know that he could care for you.
Don't ask me why someone so great would choose to walk with me and trade my
broken life for one that's new.

Go ask the child who's got a dad to love away the hurt he had before this man called
Jesus touched their lives.
God ask the one whose fears have fled, whose churning heart was quieted when
Someone whispered peace to all her strife.
Go ask the man to tell you more, whose life was just a raging war inside himself until
the Savior came.
I don't pretend to be so wise; I only know he touched my eyes and nothing else will
ever be the same.

/// A REMARKABLE RECOVERY ///

BY MIDGE DESART

how many times do we often pray and ask God to provide for our needs? The song "Go Ask" by Gloria and Bill Gaither takes me back to a time ten years earlier when my good friend, Kevin, was hospitalized because of a violent reaction to a drug. His mind was affected and doctors gave us little hope that he would recover.

My husband and I prayed often, many times in the middle of the night, and watched Kevin carefully. When he was released from the hospital, he couldn't go back to his apartment so he came to live with us. Suddenly, he was a special-needs adult. Once he had been a vibrant, funny person, but now he could barely carry on an intelligent conversation.

Music was definitely a great comfort to me during this time. God ministered healing to my soul through music.

Through this experience, the lifeline that I clung to was the knowledge that God is in control. He promised in Hebrews 13:5 that he would never leave us or forsake us.

One evening when Kevin couldn't sleep, he came across a book of God's promises that was sitting on the coffee table. Two of the helpful verses he discovered were 1 Peter 5:7, "Cast all your anxiety on him, because he cares for you" (NIV) and Hebrews 4:16, "Let us therefore come boldly unto the throne of grace, that we may obtain mercy, and find grace to help in time of need" (KJV). After reading these promises, Kevin commented, "That's a good book." He asked me to pray with him. After we prayed, the Lord had given him peace and he was able to fall asleep.

I couldn't believe my eyes the next morning when Kevin showered, dressed carefully and said he was going out to find a job. I had little hope that he would be able to find one. But I was wrong. When he returned home, Kevin said, "There's a restaurant that will hire me. I just need a note from the doctor saying it is okay for me to work, after being hospitalized."

Kevin's doctor evaluated him and told us that Kevin had made a remarkable recovery—something he rarely sees. What a joy to realize how God answered our prayers. There were many songs that came to my mind.

For ten years, there has been no sign of the devastating brain damage the doctors predicted.

In 2004, this man who had no hope of recovery recently bought his own home. One day this past summer, Kevin brought a beautiful woman to my home and introduced her as his new bride.

What does this have to do with the song that means so much to me today? The first time I heard "Go Ask," there was a sentence that spoke volumes to me. I know it speaks to many other people, as well. The song has such a special meaning.

Every time I sing the words, "Go ask the one who's burned out mind has been restored," it gives me chills to remember how God restored Kevin's mind.

MIDGE DE∫ART

Midge is a wife and mother. In addition to being an author, she is a church musician and a beading embellishment artist. She and her husband make their home in Tacoma, Washington.

THRONE OF GRACE

// WRITTEN BY SHEILA WALSH AND CHRIS EATON //

Come to the Throne of Grace
Don't be afraid
I won't turn you away
Just let me into your heart
And My love will wash your tears away

I know you
I know you completely
And on your darkest journey
I have been with you
All the weight of guilt and shame
You carry on your shoulder
It's time to hand it over and let it go
Just let it go

I can hear the silent tears
Above the noise and laughter
The things you're running after
Will let you down
So here I stand before you now
With arms of love to hold you
Let my grace enfold you
And come to Me
O run to Me

Come just come
Come

/// UNDERSTOOD GRACE ///

BY BARBARA ALBERT

my rebellion and angst played out well to the driving beat and screamed lyrics of hard rock. I locked myself in my room with my headphones on. As the decibels rose, my teenage rage at life simmered. Defeated by myself, my dark thoughts, and depression, I walked a hard path as I entered adulthood. Music followed me. It was always angrier and louder. Music played an enormous role in my life before I became a Christian.

At a point when life's crushing difficulties increased beyond my capacity to fight them or reason them away, I found salvation. Music no longer suffused me with anger sufficient to rise above trouble. I was on my own. God was working on my heart. That wore down my ability to pretend I didn't care about anything. Only then could I acknowledge my need for him and find hope and light.

I have always loved music. After I became a believer, God allowed Christian music to change me. Over the next two decades I learned to follow him. Contemporary Christian music and praise and worship intertwined at every stage of my spiritual maturity. Great healing and deeper understanding were often accompanied by lyrics in songs that seemed to be sung by the Creator Himself for me.

During phases of my spiritual growth, my musical tastes changed. For nearly a year, contemporary artist Russ Taff's raw voice echoed my own. His emotionally-charged lyrics pointed to God's truth. They also spoke my thoughts to God as a type of extended prayer. As a result, I grew and sorted out many things I had struggled with regarding my faith. Then my taste shifted to praise and worship. I listened to it exclusively as my spirit swelled with words I had never sung before. The songs made the emotions I felt inside come alive. I began singing to God of his greatness. I learned what it meant to really praise God through that type of music.

There were times when I didn't want to listen to music. I simply wanted to be quiet and study God's Word, but songs continued to flood my mind. God settled ideas in my heart in that quiet application of the music. Just the right song would come to my mind in the morning, and by afternoon, I would understand the message God was trying to get across to me. Or a song on the radio would repeat what I had been studying that week and spur me on to change and grow. I loved knowing that God cared so much about me that he gave me special messages through something I found beautiful. He carefully balanced songs with the teachings from sermons I heard and my study time. Then he faithfully tied everything together.

In recent years, however, music shifted into a different dimension for me. Four years ago, I experienced a personal crisis that I thought would kill me from a broken heart. Wracked with grief, I did nothing for weeks but cry. I saw no resolution and struggled to find God in the wreckage of broken hopes and dreams. As my shock faded, my prayers became desperate pleas for God to take away the problem and the pain.

During this time, my foundation as a Christian showed its flaws. I had built too much of my faith on religion and what was comfortable for me, but not enough on my relationship with the Lord. Before this crisis, I thought I was in good shape spiritually. But the new stresses and problems I faced dead-ended directly into my misconceptions and doubt of God. I knew I needed to come to him during this time. His grace was what I desperately needed. This could not be accomplished through my own merit or words, however. I couldn't get there on my own. It was a time when I was wrestling with my faith and with the overwhelming emotions brought about by the crisis. I prayed through my cries in the night. I thought I was headed for a nervous breakdown.

In an attempt to find peace, I attended a women's conference with some friends. I heard singer and author Sheila Walsh. Her message echoed the struggle I was going through, the struggle to accept what God freely gives on his terms, and in his way. Her honesty touched my heart. She sang beautifully at the conference. I picked up two of her CDs before going home.

I played one CD during my ride home. Sheila's ethereal voice began singing "Throne of Grace." I froze. All I could hear around me were the lyrics. It seemed as though she was standing in front of me, gently and personally beckoning me to come into the place of grace with her. As Sheila sang, some elementary understanding of God's grace for me in a place of great heartbreak dawned. I wept uncontrollably. Barriers began breaking deep inside at that moment. No one else in the car mattered. I was deeply engrossed in the song and the revelation it brought.

I played the song over and over for weeks following that night. My understanding of grace grew stronger and deeper. The understanding came slowly, but without effort on my part. The tears flowed each time I listened to the song in bed before I fell asleep. The excruciating parts of my heart that I thought was damaged forever began to heal. Changes happened inside me that I couldn't even describe. I knew they were happening because my thoughts were changing.

Every time I listened to that song, God held me in his arms and convinced me of his love. His comfort was real and present. Crossing over from the legalism I had learned from the beginning to my understanding of grace was both monumental and frightening. Each time Sheila's voice whispered God's promise to enfold me in his loving arms I grew closer to him allowing it to happen. God removed the pain of grief and comforted me as I wept away years of painful memories. I felt as if Sheila gave me the courage and boldness to go to that place through the lyrics of her song. Surely if she sang of that place so clearly, she had experienced it. I could get there, too.

I heard other songs that reinforced the call for me to give all things over to the Lord who sees every tear we shed and every grief we bear. I walked through the crisis, held up by grace as I heard Heaven's message in my ears.

Since early on in my Christian walk, I had tried everything I knew to break through to this place of grace. It took that lovely voice singing Spirit-inspired lyrics at the right time to pierce my soul and let the voice of God reach my heart. God's Word is truth. At times, however, I need to hear a message draped in beautiful harmony and orchestration to penetrate emotions that can betray my will. It was God, not me, who would take me there.

The truth that I could not embrace suddenly sprang into glorious, three-dimensional life through the song. I turned a corner in my spiritual journey and came into a fullness of my salvation. With that truth flowing through me, nothing was the same. I started a path of healing and hope in the midst of tragedy.

Just listening to 'Throne of Grace' now brings me back to that time as though it was yesterday and allows me the realization of what I nearly missed. I am who I am today because that song in God's hands transformed me.

BARBARA ALBERT

Barbara resides Grove City, Ohio. Barbara contributes to parent educator publications and teaches writing for a cooperative school.

THROUGH IT ALL

// **PERFORMED BY ANDRAE CROUCH** //

I've had many tears and sorrows.
I've had questions about tomorrow;
There've been times I didn't know right from wrong;
But in every situation God gave blessed consolation that my trials come to only make
me strong.

Chorus
Through it all, Through it all,
O I've learned to trust in Jesus, I've learned to trust in God;
Through it all, Through it all,
I've learned to depend upon his Word.

I've been to lots of places and I've seen a lot of faces,
There've been times I felt so all alone;
But in my lonely hours, yes, those precious lonely hours,
Jesus let me know that I was his own.

I thank God for the mountains And I thank him for the valleys,
I thank him for the storms he brought me through;
For if I'd never had a problem I wouldn't know that he could solve them,
I'd never know what faith in God could do."

A MOVE IN
/// THE RIGHT DIRECTION ///

BY ELAINE WRIGHT COLVIN

"**h**oney, start packing. I got the promotion and we're moving to Alaska," my husband Bob called cheerfully as he bounded in the front door of our Helena, Montana home.

My heart sunk. I wasn't ready to move again and leave all our friends. We had already lived in both Dallas and San Francisco during our five years of married life. I collapsed into the nearest chair and asked for the details?

"When? How? What about selling the house? And can we take our two foster children? How do you ship furniture to Alaska? Can I take my piano and all of my books? Yikes, don't we need a four-wheel drive truck for all of the rain and snow?" The myriad of details flashing through my mind made a very long list of questions and doubts.

"Thirty days! No way. How can we possibly be ready so soon?" I cried.

But ... the inevitable day arrived, and God worked in some surprising ways to enable us to get everything done: house sold in a week; permission from the State to take our foster boys secured after a myriad of red tape and miracles; all our earthly goods loaded into the C-van to be barged to Juneau; reservations for car and staterooms on the Alaskan ferry; and the sad goodbyes to our church family and friends.

Our last stop in Seattle before heading to the ferry dock for the Alaska Marine Highway ship, the M.V. Matanuska, was the very large and popular downtown Christian bookstore. "I'll stick my packages of new books and music into every available cubbyhole in our pickup camper—at least then I will have something to look forward to on the long Alaskan winter nights," I thought. I was already dreading the heavy rainfall I knew we were in for in Juneau.

I had only recently been introduced by my aunt Dorothy to the rich booming voice of Doug Oldham. He had fast become my favorite Gospel singer. The store had several of his new music cassettes. I bought them all. I didn't have time to listen to the demos, but it didn't matter. "His music is always an encouragement to me, so there's no way I can lose," I thought, I hurriedly paid for my stash so we could dash to get our vehicle in line for the three-day cruise to Alaska.

The ferry ride to Southeast Alaska was beautiful and calming. The kids loved watching through binoculars for the whales, eagles and other wildlife. But my thoughts rushed ahead—fearing the unknown: "Where will we live? How long will we have to be in the cramped motel room? How much will it cost us to eat out every meal? Where will we find friends and a new church to attend? Will the higher cost of living in Alaska be a killer to our budget?" I wondered.

On Monday morning in the hotel, reality set in as I stared at the rain bouncing off the window. "Here we are and my daunting tasks are just beginning," I thought to myself. Bob had to report to the office for his first day of work. I had to start looking for a place to live if I wanted to get the five of us out of that cramped motel room.

I grabbed my Bible and journal, put on my headphones and popped in a cassette to begin my morning devotions and quiet time. I only had a few minutes before the children would be waking up hungry and we'd have to head for a nearby restaurant.

"Through it all, Through it all, O I've learned to trust in Jesus, I've learned to trust in God; Through it all, Through it all, I've learned to depend upon his Word."

By now the tears were streaming down my face. "Okay, God. I'll depend on you, but the tasks ahead seem so daunting."

Flipping through my Bible, my eyes landed on Psalm 32:8, "I will instruct you and teach you in the way you should go; I will counsel you and watch over you" (NIV).

The children and I spent the first few days driving around Juneau and Douglas Island, trying to get our bearings, find a bank, a post office, a grocery store and, most importantly finding a place to live.

"Mommy, where are we going to go to school and when can we start?" five-year-old Cathy asked.

"I don't know, honey. It all depends on where God has a house for us."

I knew there weren't that many available options that we could afford. The cost of living increase in pay would hardly compensate for the higher prices that I was noticing in the stores and at the gas station. It was going to be very difficult to balance a budget here.

Each night after the kids went to sleep Bob and I poured over the real estate ads in the newspaper and made another plan of attack for my house search on the following day. Exhausted at the end of the first week of house hunting, I put on my headphones, and fell back onto my pillow: "Through it all, Through it all..."

"God, I am trying to thank you for these storms. I don't know how long it will take me to get used to sloshing through this rain. Please help us to find someplace to live, soon!"

Sunday morning was a welcome change—an opportunity to make new friends and get free advice on living in our new location. I had lots to learn: everything (clothes, food, furniture) is ordered through catalogs and takes time and planning ahead; to escape the cabin fever (a very real malady), you hop on a ferry because there are only sixteen miles of road and nowhere to go; and if you want to find excitement, you'd better make good friends and create your own fun. There weren't lots of opportunities in this '70s small town that still seemed like a gold rush frontier town.

But by mid-week, after long days and more nights in the motel, I was still crying out to God: "God, this is so hard; Learning new names and trying to keep a smile on my face. Living out of a suitcase, keeping the children entertained and waiting for the barge to arrive with our C-van and furniture...."

Tears again fell, as we turned out the light. "I've been to lots of places and I've seen a lot of faces, there've been times I felt so all alone."

"Through It All" was bringing me hope and encouragement, as well as becoming one of my all-time favorite songs (and I have been a church organist since high school).

For weeks, I clung to the promise that God would give me blessed consolation and that all the trials faced throughout this move would make me strong.

Would you be surprised to learn that God did more than I could have dreamed possible? He had a new three-bedroom duplex waiting for us. We found it just in time for the arrival of the barge bringing our belongings. We soon found the church where God wanted us to worship and serve. The friends we made there helped change our lives as we learned how important our little life inconveniences are in helping us grow up in Jesus.

For more than thirty years now (and four more major cross-country moves to Washington, D.C., Boise, Helena and Seattle), God's promises that I have held onto are in the words of this song by Andrae Crouch.

ELAINE WRIGHT COLVIN

Elaine is a popular author and speaker at Christian Writers' Conferences around the country. She and her husband just celebrated their fortieth wedding anniversary and are looking forward to retirement and spending more time with their grandchildren.

A MILLION YEARS

// PERFORMED BY THE CHOIR //

Looking forward to the day
When this pain will go away
And this hurting will have ended
Looking forward to the time
When I leave this world behind
And eternity begins
A resting place inside your arms
A resting place I'll find
And then I'll stay
A million years to be with you
A million years and more
Well, it won't be long at all
'Til at last I hear your call
And then the darkness will be ended
When the heavens open wide
And you call me to your side
Then a new life will begin
A resting place inside your arms
A resting place I will find
And then I'll stay
A Million years to be with you
A million years and more

/// NO LONGER ALONE ///

BY MARTHA YOUNG

Like almost everyone else in America, I grew up in a dysfunctional family, no fault to my parents. Among many happy times, the spirit of our lives was doused with alcoholism and pain. The four of us—my father, mother, sister and I— attended church when I was a young child; but when the congregation ousted the pastor, my father became angry and hurt. We quit going to church. My father sometimes read the Bible to us, while my sister and I looked at what we thought were scary pictures. He let us know we should revere God and his Word.

When I was a teenager, my mother took my sister and me to a Presbyterian Church for a Christmas Eve Candlelight Service. There were 15 people in the congregation. My mother became a regular attendee and my sister and I went with her on occasion.

When I was a grade-schooler, alcoholism took its hold on my family; anger and pain became the norm for us. And if I thought that was bad, detox and sobriety were worse for my father and for us, at least for a while.

As I grew older, I became depressed and developed an eating disorder. I thought often of suicide and wrote about it. Music was very important to me. I surrounded myself with depressing, introspective music that spoke to the way I felt.

After rehabilitation and three heart attacks, my father began the healing process. Our family had to go through a time of healing, too. But the aftershocks of life's trauma left me a loner. When I became old enough for college, I wanted to go far away where I knew no one. I went to a Christian College and met up with the "God Squad," Christians who wanted to save everyone. They saw me as a case. I said I wanted no part of it.

God really got through to me one night, however. My peels of laughter at the thought of God wanting me turned to great sobs as I realized I wanted him. While on my knees, I fell in love with him. I was a baby Christian. I knew nothing about Christianity. When one of my new Christian friends mentioned that he had some good Christian music, I laughed at the thought of actually liking hymns. He gave me the tapes of White Heart Hotline and Russ Taff Medals. I looked bewildered. "This is Christian music?" I asked.

My friend, Jimmy gave me a bootleg copy of Petra's "Beat the System" as a gift. I listened to it day and night. I wept every time I heard about Jesus' crucifixion while listening to "It Is Finished." I still know all the words to all three of those tapes.

When I went home during the holidays, being a Christian proved to be difficult. My old buddies thought I had gone nuts or got sucked into a cult. My family ran away from my constant and somewhat irritating preaching. Therefore, my friends became the songs on the tapes that spoke of Jesus and let me know that, like Elijah, I did not stand alone in my faith.

At college, living a Christian life was easy with all the Christians around me. But then life struck a blow. I was mortified that a family member might die. During Spring Break of the second semester of my freshman year, my father died. I was devastated. I had the strength I needed for a short while., But back at school, the thoughts of suicide came rushing back. I felt alone. While Christians said, "I understand," or "it was in God's will," I sank deeper into my loneliness. No one understood.

Hearing Youth Choir's (The Choir's) "A Millions Years" over and over pulled me through. I cannot say how many times I played that song. It helped me picture my father in Heaven, where he was healed, happy, and whole. I would one day see him again and there we would rejoice.

Since I am naturally a loner and do not trust many people, Christian music helped to shape my Christian beliefs, theology, and my concept of God. It drew me to the Bible and to prayer as no sermon could.

My mother's prayers for safety and my persistent friends' reaching out brought me to salvation. I believe the fact that I remained on that path for almost twenty years is, in part, due to Christ-centered lyrics and tunes that kept me in love with my God. They motivated me to grow in my faith, even when life proved to be difficult and when I felt all alone.

MARTHA YOUNG

Martha has been involved with Christian music since the early nineties, to include fronting the Christian rock group Asbury Lane. Martha and her husband and son live in Greenville, Illinois. She works part time at her church aiding the pastors in administrating the worship services and supporting the music department.

SOMETIMES BY STEP

// PERFORMED BY RICH MULLINS //

Sometimes the night was beautiful
Sometimes the sky was so far away
Sometimes it seemed to stoop so close
You could touch it but your heart would
  break
Sometimes the morning came too soon
Sometimes the day could be so hot
There was so much work left to do
But so much you'd already done

Chorus
Oh God, you are my God
And I will ever praise you
Oh God, you are my God
And I will ever praise you
I will seek you in the morning
And I will learn to walk in your ways
And step by step you'll lead me
And I will follow you all of my days

Sometimes I think of Abraham
How one star he saw had been lit for me
He was a stranger in this land
And I am that, no less than he
And on this road to righteousness
Sometimes the climb can be so steep
I may falter in my steps
But never beyond your reach

Chorus

And I will follow you all of my days
And I will follow you all of my days
And step by step you'll lead me
And I will follow you all of my days
And I will follow you all of my days
(Sometimes the night was beautiful)
And I will follow you all of my days
(Sometimes the night...)
(Sometimes the night was beautiful)
And I will follow you all of my days
(... Was beautiful)
(Sometimes the night was beautiful)
And I will follow you all of my days
(So beautiful)
And I will follow you all of my days
And I will follow you all of my days
(Oh God, you are my God)
And I will follow you all of my days
(Oh God, you are my God)
And I will follow you all of my days
And I will follow you all of my days
(Sometimes the night was beautiful)
And I will follow you all of my days
(Sometimes the night...)
And I will follow you all of my days"

FOLLOWING IN
GOD'S FOOTSTEPS

BY KELLEY FITZGERALD

my parents were not Christians; therefore they didn't think much about how the music they played influenced me. During the sixties and seventies, they always had music playing in our house. I grew up listening to Rock and Roll music. I knew all the words to all the songs. Many times, I would ride my bike to the local "dime store." There, I spent my allowance on 45 rpm records. I collected all the latest tunes.

I got married when I was young and started my own household. Just like my parents, we always had music playing in the house. Right about that time, in the early eighties, Music Television (MTV) was first introduced. It quickly gained popularity in households across America. We played it all the time in our house, as well.

By the time my kids were old enough to learn the words to all the popular songs and to understand the messages in the videos, I realized that the messages that were not appropriate for them were probably not good for me either.

I started attending a local church. I decided I needed to make some positive changes if I wanted to be a good example for the children, with whom God had entrusted me.

I was saved as a teenager, but was never discipled by anyone. I became involved in the church through a young adult Bible-study group. The people who were a part of that group were great examples. They helped me grow in the Lord and in his Word. Some of the people exposed me to Christian music. We went to see Rich Mullins perform at the Cincinnati Bible College. It was my first Christian concert experience.

As I grew deeper in my faith, I realized that I needed to change the music I listened to. Christian rock concerts and Christian music festivals made the transition easier for me. Through these kinds of experiences, my husband was also brought to the Lord. He asked Jesus into his heart at a Margaret Becker concert. After the concert, he shared the encounter with my pastor. He was baptized the following Sunday.

My husband was not the only one touched by the power of Christian music. It didn't take long for me to share it with my children. When my daughter was a teenager, she was exposed to the influences of popular music and she started to have some questionable tastes in recording groups. I went to a Christian bookstore and asked for a comparable alternative to the style of music to which she was listening. She listened to the CD I bought for her.

On one occasion, my daughter left her music with a non-Christian friend. The next time she was at her house, they were playing the CD and both singing along. It was great to see my daughter and her friends influenced by wholesome messages and Godly lyrics.

Christian music is a blessing to me. It is a tool that has generated Christian growth and has helped to shape my walk with Christ. Most importantly, it helps me focus more on God. It opens my heart toward God. It is one thing that can permeate deep down into our souls. Christian music touches a part of me that I believe only God should influence and control.

One example is a song that has also become my prayer. If you are at all like me, just getting to work some days can be a struggle. As I walk from the car to the building, I try to regroup before starting this part of my day. I sometimes sigh heavily and "Oh God," instinctively comes out of my mouth.

I think about how easy it would be to feel guilty or stressed, but now, without thinking the chorus to Rich Mullins's song "Sometimes by Step" immediately rolls off my tongue. I lift my hand and proclaim, "You are my God and I will ever praise you." This song has not only become my daily prayer, but a motto for my life. The song signifies exactly where I am in my walk with the Lord.

As I declare: "Oh God, you are my God and I will ever praise you,"

I am reminded that in any and all circumstances God is still God. It is my responsibility to praise him no matter what I am going through or how I am feeling.

As I continue: "I will seek you in the morning and I will learn to walk in your ways,"

It is confirmed that my walk with God is everyday. I am committing to seek him daily which requires action on my part. I need to be in his word and his presence to learn and encounter his will. I richly desire this for my life. This is where I learn to walk in his ways. I want to be that Christ-like example each day as I head to work.

While I am singing: "And step by step you'll lead me and I will follow you all of my days,"

I understand this is a process of trusting God and believing that each step of the way he is here leading me. This whole "God thing" is so personal. I am ever thankful I am rooted and have acquired the faith to follow and obey him all the days of my life. There is no doubt I am on a life long journey with my God and I am committed for the long haul. To me, this song sums it all up. It is where I am and where I feel I should be.

If Rich Mullins had not recorded this song, and if Christian radio stations had not played it frequently, I wouldn't have this as my prayer today. The song focuses my attention to my all-powerful, all-loving God, rather than on the stress that I could have easily consumed me.

KELLEY L. FITZGERALD

Kelley is a full-time wife and mother and part-time computer analyst. She has two grown children, two granddaughters, and two school-age boys. She and her family are very active in Lebanon, Ohio.

BREATHE

// WRITTEN BY MARIE A. BARNETT //

This is the air I breathe,
This is the air I breathe,
Your Holy presence living in me.

This is my daily bread,
This is my daily bread,
Your very Word spoken to me.

And I, I'm desperate for you.
And I, I'm lost without you.

LEARNING TO BREATHE AGAIN

BY KAREN DECOSTA

ave you ever had to depend on the Lord to give you the desires of your heart? My husband and I had to wait on the Lord for our children. We have had to trust him through the hardships and uncertainties we have faced.

My husband and I met at a Southern Baptist college, Charleston Southern University. We graduated together the same year. After we were married, we tried to have children. After only a few months, I found out I was pregnant. Within a week after I found out I was pregnant, however, I had a miscarriage. That was very difficult.

I had heard about many other women who had miscarried during their first pregnancy. I tried to keep a positive attitude, thinking that this would only happen to me once.

We wanted to have children so we continued to try. The next year, we consulted a doctor. With proper medication, we found ourselves expecting again. Unfortunately, this pregnancy resulted in my second miscarriage. This time, I had put too much confidence in the doctor to ensure a successful pregnancy. This loss made me feel empty, both emotionally and spiritually.

I went through times feeling like I did not want to be in church or listen to music. Nor did I want to be around pregnant women.

A few weeks after our loss, my husband and I were scheduled to go to a yearly conference for pastors and their wives. At this conference, the band ministered to me. During the first couple of songs, I poured my heart out to God, as I was singing and praying that God would heal me.

I closed my eyes, sang to the Lord, and lifted my hands in humble worship. While singing, I confessed to God. I also recognized that he was in total control. I knew my life was not merely in the control of my doctor. I asked for forgiveness because I felt that I was looking for joy in my circumstances rather than in finding completed joy in my relationship with God.

During that time, I was also dealing with depression. The song "Breathe" brought me great comfort. I had to seek God and allow him to deliver me from the disappointment and the pain that I experienced when I had the second miscarriage. When I was desperate to have a child, I needed to be desperate for God. I needed to learn to "breathe" again.

My husband and I really wanted children, and even after the second miscarriage, we kept trying. We had three miscarriages. We tried to conceive through insemination several times. That procedure wasn't successful either. We tried to adopt three times prior to the successful adoption of our two children, Luke and Morgan.

Initially, we were only going to adopt a baby boy who had not yet been born. His sister was two at the time. The baby's mother changed her mind right after the birth, however, in September of 1999. Then we got a call in December of 1999, asking if we would take both of the children. We quickly agreed. The children immediately went into foster care, and on March 3, 2000, they became ours.

The adoption was a blessing for the children, but it was more of a blessing to us. We had prayed and tried to have children, but there were so many disappointments. We wondered what God was doing. There were people who didn't need to have children. We had a good marriage and our relationship with the Lord was strong.

"Well, maybe God still has something to teach us and maybe that is why he hasn't given us children," we reasoned.

We were right. God taught us many things through those miscarriages, and through the adoptions that didn't go through. God taught us that our joys in life need to come from our relationship with him and not from our circumstances. We learned that we need to be content in life as it is. We also learned to be satisfied with what we had and not long for the things we don't have.

Satan tries to have us believe his lies. He tries to discourage us from following the Lord as we face trials. He would like to see us not being satisfied, never finding contentment, and always wanting more.

Now, I praise the Lord that I went through those hardships. I don't know if I would have learned these valuable lessons otherwise.

Since that time, God has continually taught me to depend on him. He has drawn me to worship on a daily basis, that I can remain focused on serving and praising him.

Being a pastor's wife is a blessing. I have the opportunity to minister to so many people. Sometimes, I meet people in our ministry who have gone through similar situations. I am able to share what we went through in our experience. It helps by giving them hope.

I explain that being a parent is the most selfless thing that we can do. This is not something selfish that we are asking for. God puts the desire to be parents in our hearts. I tell them to praise the Lord for that desire and to ask the Lord to help prepare them for parenthood.

Then I explain that we should pray without ceasing, knowing that God will answer all of our prayers in his time. And when it seems that our prayers go unanswered, he is right there, sustaining us, just as the air we breathe.

KAREN DECOSTA

Karen and her husband have been married and working in ministry for sixteen years. Now she performs the most rewarding job ever, raising their two children.

PEACE SPEAKER

// **WRITTEN BY GERON DAVIS** //

It was such a lovely day.
The sun was shining bright.
The gentle winds were blowing my way.
Not a storm cloud was in sight.

Then suddenly, without warning,
A storm surrounded my life.
But even in the storm
I could feel a calm,
And here's the reason why.

I know the Peace Speaker,
I know him by name.
I know the Peace Speaker,
He controls the wins and waves.
When he says "Peace be still."
They have to obey.
I know the Peace Speaker.
Yes, I know him by name.

There's never been another man
With the power of this man.
By simply saying "Peace be still."
He can calm the strongest wind.

And that's why I never worry
When the storm clouds come my way.
I know that he is near
To drive away my fears
And I can smile and say...

I know the Peace Speaker,
I know him by name.
I know the Peace Speaker.
He controls the winds and waves.
When he says "Peace be still."
They have to obey.
I know the Peace Speaker,
Yes I know him by name

Peace, peace, wonderful peace.
Coming down from the Father above.
When he says "Peace be still."
They have to obey.
I'm glad I know the Peace Speaker.
Yes, I know him by name.
I'm glad I can say,
I know the Peace Speaker.
Yes I know him by name."

THE LORD MET ME AT MY NEED

BY JOY JONES

I was raised in a loving family. I learned to love the Lord. I could never imagine going to prison for something I didn't do, or for a crime I didn't commit. But, at forty-eight years of age, I spent three years in prison for something I didn't do. It was devastating. I felt like the Lord had left the building. My life was instantly turned upside down. I was spinning out of control.

In prison, there were girls from all walks of life. They came in all colors, shapes and sizes. They were prostitutes, murderers, drug dealers, and users. There were also girls there who were innocent.

In prison, there is no respecter of persons. We were all grouped together. There were six or eight of us to a room.

I felt all alone in the crowd. I wondered if the Lord could even hear me. How did this happen? I was a Christian serving time in prison. It was bad enough when I lost my friends and family. And to top it off, I was living with criminals.

To make matters worse, I had a roommate that was involved with another inmate. "You can't get rid of me. I told you that you were mine," Sheila said to Lena, as they both came into our room. Sheila had followed my roommate Lena into our room from her building across the yard.

"Sheila, just leave me alone." Lena said.

"I'll leave you alone when I'm good and ready." Sheila snarled as she threw Lena over her shoulder and walked out of the room.

"Could this really be happening or am I having a bad dream?" I wondered. I had never seen anything like that before. I was afraid of Sheila and afraid for Lena.

About a week later, the two had made up and Sheila was back. It was very uncomfortable when she was in the room. There was something quite evil about her.

It was a day like all the rest. I was sitting on my bed writing letters, doing some drawing, and listening to Christian music. The sun was shining and things seemed to be as good as they could be in prison.

At five minutes to the hour, the doors were unlocked. They stayed open for fifteen minutes. The doors clicked and in walked Sheila. She was a tall woman that walked, talked, and looked like a man.

Sheila was often a self-imposed guest in our room. She would barge in at times when we were dressing, bathing, or in the bathroom. The shower and toilet doors were doors with open spaces at the top and bottom. There was very little privacy. Sheila saw to it that we had no privacy.

When she walked in, she never spoke to any of us. That day her rudeness was more than I could take. I knew no one else in the room liked it either, but they would never say anything to her. I guess I lost my cool.

"Sheila, you come in whenever you want to. It doesn't matter what we are doing. You aren't even supposed to be in here. You need to stay out," I demanded.

She never uttered a sound; she simply turned around and walked out. I thought I handled that all right. Nothing was said about the incident that evening. The room had a good feeling. Everyone was joking and laughing.

The next day, however, I came in from work and saw Sheila come out of my room. "Oh no, she's at it again," I thought.

She walked straight towards me, looked down and said, "You need to remember what I'm here for." Then she walked off. My heart began to pound, I was sure everyone could hear it.

Everyone knew that she was there for setting a woman on fire. She had just recently gotten out of a two year lockdown for pouring perfume on an inmate and trying to set fire to her. I cannot explain the stark fear I felt. It was the only time while I was incarcerated that I feared for my life.

I tried to stay out of her way, even though it was difficult. She was trying hard to make it her job to constantly be in my path. She would follow me if I went to the yard to walk on the track. She worked in the chow hall. She smiled wickedly at me when I went through the line. The remainder of the week, I prayed and cried until there were no more tears. The walk to and from my work assignment everyday became my prayer trail. I cried and prayed all the way. I didn't feel God's presence. Even though the room was locked, I had trouble sleeping. No one ever asked me what was wrong but I think they all knew. Rumors went around very quickly.

On Thursday, I was in my prison office doing some paper work at my job. I was getting settled in, when in walked Sergeant Z.

"Okay, out with it. What's going on?" he asked. I tried to assure him that everything was all right. Sergeant Z closed the door, walked over to me and laid his hand on my shoulder and said, "Tell me."

At that point, I fell apart. I told him the whole story of Sheila invading our space and threatening me. " I'm so sorry," he said, "I'd like to hug you, but I can't. You know prison rules."

Then he quickly hugged me and added softly, "You know the 'Peace Speaker,' and you won't get hurt." "Peace Speaker" was a song on a tape that I had been listening to. I loved the words but it had never meant more than it did that day.

Sgt. Z could be very gruff when he needed to be, but I found out that day how caring and compassionate he was, as well. It felt good to tell someone…but what if Sheila found out about it? What would she do? This could get worse.

The following Saturday, I was the only inmate to work outside the gate. My duty was to help the officer put families in the family visiting units. Then I could go back to my room. Sergeant Z was usually on duty Saturday. He would take me to the gate, let me through the Sally Port, and then I would go on alone. He was supposed to pat me down, but he just let me through that day. "Take care, kid. Remember The Peace Speaker," he reminded me, as he let me out. He had tried to cheer me up. It was hard to act normal. I was so scared I felt numb.

As I walked behind all the buildings to get to my yard, I was crying so hard I couldn't see through the tears. I felt I was at the end of my rope and there was nowhere to go but down. I stopped, raised my arms to the Lord and cried, "Lord, where are you?"

"What if someone sees me?" I thought. Opening my eyes, I saw a mass of fluttering orange coming towards me. It was difficult to focus through the tears. Orange butterflies landed all over me. There had to be at least 300 to 500 of them. The feeling was indescribable. I felt warmth, peace, love, joy, and safety.

I don't know how long the butterflies remained on me. It could have been five seconds, ten minutes, or an hour. When they fluttered away that "peace that passes all understanding" remained with me. I knew that the Lord was with me. Even though I was an innocent person spending time in prison with some unsavory characters, everything was going to be all right.

The walk back to my room was wonderful. The birds were singing, the sun was shining, and all was well with my soul. The Peace Speaker was truly with me.

When I went back into my block unit I heard a lot of commotion. "Have you heard?" someone said. "Sheila has been sent back to lockdown." My mouth dropped open as I shook my head in surprise and disbelief. They had put her back into the secure unit for something else she had done. She remained there until after I was released. Thank you, Lord.

The next day I was on my way to chapel. I passed Sergeant Z. He winked and said, "It's a beautiful morning, isn't it?" It was a very beautiful morning!

JOY JONES

Joy has traveled the world and has aspirations to write a book. She spent three years in prison for a crime she didn't commit. She and her husband of ten years are retired, and they spend their time making crafts.

GOD OF WONDERS

// PERFORMED BY CAEDMON'S CALL //

Lord of heaven and earth.
Lord of all creation.
Lord of heaven and earth.

Lord of all creation,
of water, earth and sky.
The heavens are your Tabernacle.
Glory to the Lord on high!

God of wonders beyond our galaxy,
you are holy, holy.
The universe declares your majesty,
you are holy, holy.

Lord of heaven and earth
Lord of heaven and earth

Early in the morning,
I will celebrate the light.
When I stumble in the darkness,
I will call your name by night

God of wonders beyond our galaxy,
you are holy, holy.
The universe declares your majesty,
you are holy, holy.

Lord of heaven and earth
Lord of heaven and earth

Hallelujah, to the Lord of heaven and
    earth (3x)

holy, holy

God of wonders beyond our galaxy,
you are holy, holy.
Precious Lord, reveal your heart to me,
you are holy, holy.
The universe declares your majesty,
you are holy, holy.

holy, holy

Hallelujah to the lord of heaven and
    earth (6x)

GOD REMINDS ME
/// OF HIS WONDER ///

BY SUZANNE GUTIERREZ-HEDGES

do you ever feel like you need a miracle? I believe God is in the business of performing miracles. I don't think that he always reveals his wonders in the ways we typically expect, however. What I appreciate the most is seeing God work in my own life. God works things out the way he wants. It causes my faith to grow as I watch him do just that.

I am an aspiring actress. My goal is to one day have my own sitcom. To become an actor or actress, one must be proactive and motivated and have a high self-esteem. He or she must be able to take constructive criticism and be able to handle rejection.

There are a lot of people in Hollywood and in Los Angeles, who think that they are better than others. We might meet people who we think are friends, but find out quickly that they have a totally different mentality. They have the "what can you do for me?" attitude.

Life in California can be a challenge since that attitude is the opposite of how God wants us to be. It is hard to meet Christian people there. I have prayed that God would place me in the presence of Christian people. Therefore, I have met a few. I want to be with Christian people who have the same aspirations that I have. I would like to associate with those who have positive characteristics of good actors or actresses without the "backstabbing" or the "what can you do for me attitude."

There are so many people in the film and television industry who are quick to tell you about their accomplishments. "Listen to what I've done," or "I've done this, and I've done that."

I believe that it is God's power and wonder that is paving the way for me as I meet my career goals and fulfill my dreams.

There are things in Hollywood that bring bright spots of hope. Mel Gibson brought hope with "The Passion of the Christ."

I have been blessed to have good Christian friends help me through all of the tough times. I have also been involved in groups where no one else in the group is a Christian. I was part of a production company filled with nonbelievers for a long time until I finally left.

"Does God want me to witness to these people?" or "is this Satan trying to challenge me in my Christian walk?" I asked myself those questions many times. I found that I had to seek God in everything. God said "go" and therefore I left.

There are certain roles I won't audition for and certain projects I won't take on because of my values and because of what I believe. If there is a part that includes nudity, I won't do it. If I am auditioning for a role where there is swearing, I choose not to curse. I don't think it is necessary. There are plenty of other adjectives that can be used to communicate the same messages.

I don't necessarily go into a room and proclaim "I'm a Christian." I think people can see the fruits of a Godly lifestyle through the choices I make and how I conduct myself in various situations. I don't go into a room and say, "I am a girl," either but I think my actions and how I respond to things would allow them to see the kind of person I am.

I think it is better not to compromise, even if it means not taking a role, or if it means being in a less-than-Godly situation.

When I hear the words of "God of Wonders," it always reminds me to put God first – in my decisions, my career choices, and in everything I do.

God is continuing to teach me to depend on him. In the last year and a half, I have been studying the Bible more often. I am active in a Bible study. My friends, in my Bible-study group, share how God has done miraculous things in people's lives. That has been an inspiration to me.

I see God's wonders more in the every day events and by the way he always makes a way for me. I just auditioned for a Christian theater company, and was accepted. I am very excited about it. I am now in a theatrical group made up of Christians.

I have seen God at work in my own life, both in my career and in my personal Christian walk. It means a lot to me to be able to see God's wonders in our every day lives, even at times when we might expect them the least.

SUZANNE GUTIERREZ-HEDGES

Suzanne currently resides in Los Angeles, where she works as a freelance graphic designer and actress.

HEALING RAIN

// PERFORMED BY MICHAEL W. SMITH //

Healing rain is coming down
It's coming nearer to the old town
Rich and poor, weak and strong
It's bringing mercy, it won't be long

Healing rain is coming down
It's coming closer to the lost and found
Tears of joy and tears of shame
Are washed forever in Jesus' name

Chorus:
Healing rain it comes with fire
So let it fall and take us higher
Healing rain, I'm not afraid
To be washed in Heaven's rain

Lift your heads, let us return
To the mercy seat where time began
And in your eyes I see the pain
Come soak this dry heart with healing rain

And only you, the Son of man
Can take a leper and let him stand
So lift your hands, they can be held
By someone greater, the Great I am
Healing rain is falling down
Healing rain is falling down
I'm not afraid
I'm not afraid"

Words by Michael W. Smith, Martin Smith, and Matt
Bromleewe. © 2004 Word Music, Inc. / SmittyFly Music
/ ASCAP (admin. by Word Music, Inc.) / Curious? Music
UK / PRS (admin in United States and Canada by EMI
CMG Publishing) / Songs from the Farm / BMI (admin. by
Windswept Pacific). All Rights reserved. Used by permission.

/// I'M NOT AFRAID ///

BY KAREN HAWLEY

will never forget the most important day of my life. It was in June 1970. I was nine years old. I remember exactly where I was, who was with me, what was foremost on my mind and even what I was wearing. I knew what I had to do and I was more than willing and ready to do it. I was born for that day—a day that would set the stage for every day thereafter and become the landmark of my existence.

I was sitting in a pew at Westside Baptist Church in Cincinnati, Ohio. My mom was sitting beside me. My mom is and always has been my dearest and closest friend. I have always loved her, respected her immensely, and held her in the highest esteem. But at that time, I believed the lie that it just wasn't cool to sit with your parents. I wanted to sit with my friends.

I was wearing a tan dress with flowers on it and short sleeves with lace. It was a dress that my mom and I had picked out together during one of our special shopping escapades to the mall. Going shopping with my mom for our Sunday morning dresses is one of my fondest childhood memories.

I was waiting for the invitation hymn to begin and for Brother Wainscott to make his altar call. To this day, I get tickled as I can still hear him say... "Will you do it? Will you do it? Will you do it?" He would always say it just that way, three times over. My knees were shaking like chattering teeth and the beads of sweat were starting to trickle down my face. My heart was ready, but apparently my legs were not. I was nervous, but unafraid.

It was a no-brainer, however. As the invitation hymn began and the pastor's words cried out "Will you do it?" I would answer "yes" and commit my life to Jesus. I managed to stand up and make it to that altar, shaky legs and all. The sweat beads didn't matter, as the pool of tears washed down my face. I sobbed in both repentance and gratitude to God for sending his Son, Jesus, to die for me and save me from my sin.

At nine, I had no idea just how grateful I would become for that amazing gift of grace. I had no idea at the physical and spiritual battles I would face in the years to come and how much sin I would need to be forgiven for. Now, at 44, I am well aware.

Even at such a young age, I was on fire for God. My mom and grandparents faithfully took me to church on Sunday mornings and Sunday nights. Looking back, I would probably say we were at church just about every other night, as well.

It was in church that my love for Christian music began. At that same time, I began taking classical piano lessons that ultimately allowed me the opportunity to play the piano for Vacation Bible School each summer. I joined the choir and loved singing the hymns, like "He Lives" and "Amazing Grace." I especially remember every Easter singing "Christ the Lord Has Risen Today." This was also my first experience in being part of a youth group, which I loved. It was with that youth group, at a Saturday night youth rally, that I was introduced to my very first contemporary Christian song, "I Wish We'd All Been Ready," by Larry Norman.

I always felt God's presence in my life. Even as a small child, I loved him and pursued intimacy with him. I already knew the power of his resurrection and might and the pleasure of his presence. There was never any question in my mind but that God was real and that Jesus died for me. I knew that the Holy Spirit would help me through anything in this life.

I remember reading the Bible daily at a very young age; even though I couldn't understand a lot of the words I was reading. I knew deep within my heart that it was true and pure and wholly inspired. I realized that it would be my guidebook for living, even my sword.

It was also in those very early years, that Christian music became a driving force in my walk with God. At the time, I had no idea that this same Christian music would become one of the greatest weapons of my warfare.

Neither did I know I was going to need all the help I could get to face the oncoming troubles, which were bound to come. Each of them would be opportunities for fear to creep in and make my heart its home. And, as I expected, storms came my way.

I will never forget the night when my dad brought me home after a weekend visit with him and his new wife. My mom and dad divorced when I was two years old. He and my mom began fighting over me outside of my bedroom. I immediately grabbed my small white Bible and clutched it to my heart, as I bowed on my knees in prayer, sobbing uncontrollably.

During my junior high years, there was a new kind of trouble simmering. There were many occasions where physical fights would break out after school. When I was in seventh grade during study hall a group of ninth grade girls, who loved to cause trouble, waited for the teacher to leave the room and then proceeded to surround my desk. I was holding that same small white Bible., I used it to write scripture verses or sayings such as "Jesus loves you" on slips of colored paper that I would drop in lockers in between classes. One of the girls, Jean, asked me if I was a "Jesus freak." I thought for a moment and told her unequivocally that "Yes, I am a Jesus freak."

All of these girls were much bigger than me. My first thought was, "These girls are going to crush me." I was tempted to let fear set in, but was actually proud that they attached the "Jesus freak" label to me. When they saw that I wasn't afraid and actually had a smile on my face, they backed away from me and didn't say another word. I count that day as a victory.

These days, the troubles are even more ferocious, in greater magnitude, and come with a vengeance. They bring with them even more temptation for fear to reign over my life instead of faith. And just when I think I have overcome one battle, there is another one not too far down the road.

For example, this year my mom was diagnosed with colon cancer. This was probably the most devastating news I have ever had to face. I was completely unprepared. I was distraught. I was afraid.

My mom, along with the church and God's Word, taught me to live in love and not be afraid. It is my mom who showed me what that same fearlessness and God-like love looks like in real life. It is my mom who taught me first hand the power of living free and the power of forgiveness.

My mom had surgery to remove the cancerous mass. She was in and out of the hospital several times due to complications and infection. I will never forget the day I called 911. I watched her sink into a deep dark depression and, for a long period of time, all she could do was cry. She had not recovered from the loss of her mother when her battle with cancer began.

Immediately after the surgery and after a short time of recovery, the doctors advised Mom to have chemotherapy. She was adamant not to take that road. I wrestled with God and also within myself for answers, weighing the potential outcomes of her decision. I was afraid.

In the midst of this battle with cancer and the inner struggle to overcome fear and doubt with faith and trust, the hospital bills continued to stack up. Of course, fear is always waiting in the wings to proclaim, "your troubles are insurmountable—you might as well give up – your life is over."

With our natural eye, the tragedies of our life circumstance seem overwhelming. While initially facing this crisis I wanted to isolate myself from everyone and everything. I wanted to run to God and beat his door down, pleading for his healing rain, for a miracle.

There were days when I felt completely numb. Satan flooded my mind with visions of the cancer living inside my mom's body, wreaking havoc, and spreading its venom throughout.

I was weary, tired, teetering on the edge of a breakdown. I could feel my faith drifting off to sleep. I was weak from the fight. I became more and more afraid. I was afraid that the worse was headed our way, afraid my mom's spirit would break under the pressure, afraid I would have a breakdown, afraid I would lose my mom too soon and afraid to face tomorrow.

What I needed was a miracle... a miracle rain coming down out of Heaven, washing away the cancer, the pain, the doubt, and the fear.

Then I heard Michael W. Smith's song "Healing Rain." That song awakened my faith. It all made sense once again... the tragedy and the triumph, the joy and the pain, his mercy and his power... and just like the deer panting for the water, I was thirsty for God's healing rain to come. It came. It's here.

KAREN HAWLEY

Karen resides in Cincinnati. She is a member of the Presidential Prayer Team and the Gospel Music Association.

I HAVE DECIDED
TO FOLLOW JESUS

// UNKNOWN //

I have decided to follow Jesus;
I have decided to follow Jesus;
I have decided to follow Jesus;
No turning back, no turning back.

Though I may wonder, I still will follow;
Though I may wonder, I still will follow;
Though I may wonder, I still will follow;
No turning back, no turning back.

The world behind me, the cross before me;
The world behind me, the cross before me;
The world behind me, the cross before me;
No turning back, no turning back.

Though none go with me, still I will follow;
Though none go with me, still I will follow;
Though none go with me, still I will follow;
No turning back, no turning back.

Will you decide now to follow Jesus?
Will you decide now to follow Jesus?
Will you decide now to follow Jesus;
No turning back, no turning back.

Unknown. Public Domain

PUTTING MY FAITH
IN ACTION

/// ///

BY TODD DANIEL

a s we embarked on our first missionary experience, my wife, Jennifer, and I had high hopes of ministering to the people of Nigeria. Prior to leaving the United States, we had no idea that there was such opposition between the Christians and the Muslims. We definitely didn't expect the fighting to break out among us.

I thought we had done everything possible to prepare us for the journey ahead. We went through training at Valley of Praise in Idaho and worked for two years preparing to live as missionaries abroad. My wife and I went to Nigeria, thinking we would spend the rest of our lives there. We arrived at the Kano, Nigeria, airport on January 6, 1992. The airport was full of military police with machine guns, as well as, thousands of Muslim pilgrims going Mecca.

We had only spent about four months in Nigeria before we faced a day that I will never forget. Fighting broke out between the Muslims and the Christians in the capitol city, Jalingo.

There was a series of little villages spread across the countryside, with grass huts and a few mortar buildings. It was a Friday which started out like any other typical day. We woke up early and had breakfast, which consisted of eggs and fried doya (something like a three-foot long potato). After breakfast my good friend, Jonathon, a native Mumuyan, and I took off into the bush. We went far back into the bush to the Mumuyan evangelists and their wives.

Before Jonathon and I left our home that morning, we said our goodbyes to our wives and set off for our meeting with the evangelist. Upon arriving in the village, the people were always excited and glad to see us. The children would shout "batarde" with excitement, which meant "white man." There were only about a half a dozen white people in the area where we were. Many of the natives had never seen a white person before.

We spent a couple of hours there in praise and worship, while ministering to the people. Then we would travel back home to our wives. As we set out to return in our small Toyota bush truck, we went approximately two miles before coming to a small town along the road. It was there that we began to see our faith in God in action.

Since there are few paved roads in the bush of Nigeria, the road we had to take went past the capital of Jalingo. As we drove, we noticed that the people who lived there were running around frantically. As we approached, the mailman told us not to go any further because the Muslims and the Christians were fighting in Jalingo.

The fighting broke out in the schoolyard. It spread from there to the churches. The Muslims tried to attack and burn down the churches. My first response was shock, and then I was struck with fear. I had not planned on something like this happening. As I looked into Jonathon's eyes, I could see he was very concerned, as well.

At that point, we had two choices. We could stay where we were until the fighting stopped or we would drive right through it so we could make sure our families were safe. We really didn't have a choice at all. Our wives were at the compound and we agreed that we had to go back and make sure they were safe. Jonathon also had children in school where the fighting broke out. We chose to drive right through the fighting.

One traditional hymn kept going through my mind "I have decided to follow Jesus, no turning back, no turning back." Those words became so real that I was made to realize the true magnitude of the words penned in the song.

The Nigerians had built a roadblock of old junk cars and boards with nails sticking straight up. They placed these items all the way across the road. When we got to that place, the road was blocked and fires were being lit. We witnessed people being persecuted and killed as we drove through. They were pouring gas on people and then burning them. I drove off the side of the road and went through the bush. We stayed off the main road for the entire drive back and drove through doya fields. When we made it back to the compound, our wives had no idea that the fighting was going on.

I remember how we sang the song together at the top of our lungs. It brought us peace, knowing that God was going to see us through that terrifying experience. Many people, both Muslims and Christians, were killed that day and also in the days that followed.

We were only in Jalingo six months before we were repatriated. They thought we were American spies. When the war broke out, Immigration called us in. They told us that we had to leave the country. When the fighting broke out, we realized it was time to go.

We had waited for three years before we actually went over. We never understood exactly why this happened since we had totally committed our lives to serving God through missionary work. God had brought it about. He had provided the funds and everything that we needed. While we were there, however, we helped get the Bible translated into the language of the Mumuyan people. That was probably the greatest accomplishment we made.

The day of the fighting, the song "I Have Decided To Follow Jesus" clearly reminded me how faithful God is. He was faithful in safely bringing us through the fighting and back to our families. I was also reminded of Paul and Silas, as they lay there in prison, singing and praising God. God responded by delivering them to safety.

The reassuring words of "I Have Decided To Follow Jesus" helped me to realize that music not only helps us as we praise God, but it can also help us through times when we are tried and tested. Music tells me that the will of God will not take us where the grace of God cannot keep us.

TODD DANIEL

Todd and his wife and two children live in Madison Township, Ohio, where he is the Roads Superintendent and a member of school board.

WHO AM I

// **PERFORMED BY CASTING CROWNS** //

Who am I?
That the Lord of all the earth,
Would care to know my name,
Would care to feel my hurt,
Who am I?
That the Bright and Morning Star,
Would choose to light the way,
For my ever wandering heart,

Not because of who I am,
But because of what you've done,
Not because of what I've done,
But because of who you are,

I am a flower quickly fading,
Here today and gone tomorrow,
A wave tossed in the ocean (ocean),
A vapor in the wind,
Still you hear me when I'm calling,
Lord, you catch me when I'm falling,
And you've told me who I am..
I am Yours.

Who am I?
That the eyes that see my sin,
Would look on me with love,
and watch me rise again,
Who am I?
That the voice that calmed the sea,
Would call out through the rain,
And calm the storm in me,

Not because of who I am,
But because of what you've done,
Not because of what I've done,
But because of who you are,

I am a flower quickly fading,
Here today and gone tomorrow,
A wave tossed in the ocean (ocean),
A vapor in the wind,
Still you hear me when I'm calling,
Lord, you catch me when I'm falling,
And you've told me who I am...
I am Yours, I am Yours.

I am Yours,
Whom shall I fear?
Whom shall I fear?
'Cause I am Yours,
I am Yours."

CHANGE WILL
/// DO YOU GOOD ///

BY CAROLYN JONES

have you ever experienced a time when you had to trust God as you experienced a major change in your life? I learned to trust God in times of change. He has always had his best for me in mind and works out all the details in every situation in my life.

Over the past few years, I have been going through several drastic changes. Many of these changes occurred at the same time. I had to learn to depend on God to carry me through each situation, to ease my anxiety, calm my fears, and to ultimately work out his plan for his glory.

I am 37 years old and the mother of three children. I had always wanted to become a teacher. I loved the idea of teaching, but I never felt like I had the courage to pursue the profession.

I recently decided to make a mid-life career change and to fulfill my dream of becoming a teacher. I was apprehensive about all the things I had to do to prepare myself for this kind of change. I was anxious about student teaching and also about finding a job.

I did my student teaching during the 2001/2002 school year. I taught in two different schools as a part of the criteria for my graduate program. One school was situated in an urban setting and the other was in a suburban neighborhood. Being a minority in the system was frightening, but the students were accepting of me and saw my caring attitude toward them. We got along great.

I witnessed God as he worked out the details of my decision. I was offered a job just a few days before school started in a rural setting. When I started the job I had concerns about the new position. I wondered if it would go well and if I would be well received by the children.

I put everything in God's hands and trusted him to work out every detail.

I thought about how awesome God's power is, and how wonderful it is that he is able to do all of the things he does in the world.

I focused on the fact that he knows our hearts' desires, our wants and needs, and that he is able to care for us individually. He never overlooks the smallest care or concern we have. He gives us the strength to handle every problem we encounter in this life. I see evidence of this in my own life every day.

I faced a lot of fears as I made the career change. The song "Who Am I" helped to give me hope and assurance during a time when I felt like everything in my life was being challenged.

I was baptized as a child, but as I grew up, I realized that I needed to have a more personal relationship with God. At the age of 23, I renewed my commitment to Christ. But even then, I felt like the enemy was trying to interfere in my Christian walk. I felt his spiritual attacks as they challenged my growth. I talked to my pastor and my long-time friend about some of the situations I was going through.

My faith continued to grow and by the time I was thirty, I felt like things were different. I grew up, had children and could see the changes that had taken place in my life over the years. My faith became more and more real. I knew I needed God to get me through the difficulties I was going through. Even though I felt like I was making positive decisions for my life, I wanted God to be there and hear all of them.

As I was embarked on my new career, in a new setting, I hoped that everything would work out. God made it happen. The chorus of the song gave me the confidence that I needed to get through all of the challenges I faced. "I am Yours, Whom shall I fear? Whom shall I fear? 'Cause I am Yours, I am Yours."

As the sun comes up each morning, I listen to "Who Am I" as I drive to work. It is a worshipful experience for me.

Everything surrounding the change went smoothly. God revealed Himself at every turn. Things worked out perfectly. I put my faith in him and he has always been there for me. Even through times when I felt like he wasn't there, God revealed Himself to me.

God has given me many opportunities to share my faith with other people regarding the things he has done in my life. I just emailed a friend who was dealing with a death and gave them the words to "Who Am I" in hopes that it would be an inspiration to them. I hoped it would give her the strength to get her through her loss. God is so powerful and he listens to each one of us. He knows us and loves us so much.

The lyrics say, "I am a flower quickly fading, here today, and gone tomorrow." I used to have the idea that we are just a blink in the eye of the universe, as far as time goes. People get so caught up in materialism and in making big choices, which are really distractions. But, the words proclaim that God will hear everything we have to say because he knows our thoughts and our deepest concerns.

God continues to show me that life's changes are good. I am a first year teacher. God continually lets me know he is there by helping and guiding me. I have amazed myself, both inside the classroom and outside by managing a busy schedule and hectic lifestyle. I know beyond a shadow of a doubt that I could not have done this on my own and that I need God's help.

CAROLYN JONES

Carolyn resides in Wilmington, Ohio, with her husband of nine years, two boys and a baby girl. She teaches eighth-grade English in a small, rural school district.

AMAZING GRACE

// **WRITTEN BY JOHN NEWTON** //

Amazing Grace! How sweet the sound
That saved a wretch like me!
I once was lost, but now am found
Was blind, but now I see.

'Twas Grace that taught my heart to fear,
And Grace my fears relieved.
How precious did that Grace appear
The hour I first believed.

Through many dangers, toils, and snares
I have already come.
'Tis Grace hath brought me safe thus far
And Grace will lead me home.

The Lord has promised good to me.
His Word my hope secures.
He will my shield and portion be
As long as life endures.

When we've been there ten thousand years
Bright shining as the sun,
We've no less days to sing God's praise
Than when we'd first begun.

Words by John Newton. Public Domain

/// WE ARE GOD'S FAMILY ///

BY W.C. MARTIN

my wife, Donna and I took a great leap of faith one day in 1996. After the death of her mother, Donna felt that she needed to fill to the void that the loss of her mother left. We prayed together about something that the Lord had placed on Donna's heart. The Lord spoke to us. He told us to adopt children.

We already had two biological children of our own. We adopted four other children, all of whom came from broken homes. Bennett Chapel Missionary Baptist Church, which is made up of about 200 members, has since adopted over 70 children, as well.

Although Donna's mother, Murtha Cartwright, died in February 1996, her love lives on through the lives of these children. Murtha gave birth to seventeen children. She loved each one with an unconditional kind of love.

When Donna and I prayed together we felt the Lord giving us a message, "What about the children that don't have what you had in a mother?" He said, "Give it back to a child—foster and adopt."

Initially, we never tried to convince anyone else to adopt. The inspiration of our story, however, has initiated a chain reaction in our predominately African American congregation in Shelbyville, Texas. Many families have followed our lead. One verse that reinforces our mission is Mark 10:14, "Let the little children come to me, and do not hinder them, for the kingdom of God belongs to such as these" (NIV).

We especially feel motivated to adopt African-American children, because Texas, one of many states, has a disproportionate number of African-American children who need to be adopted. The members of our church have adopted mostly "special needs" children. These children are very difficult to place. The church offers support groups for parents who face the challenges associated with children with specific behavior and developmental issues. Many of these children suffer from exposure to drugs. Many were either born drug-addicted or endured the abuse of drug-addicted parents. They may also suffer from irritability, developmental delays, and psychological issues related to separation and loss.

The song "Amazing Grace" demonstrates how God's power is working in our church. The words, "Amazing Grace! How sweet the sound, that saved a wretch like me. I once was lost, but now am found, was blind, but now I see," have such an awesome meaning to me, because it was God's unmerited grace and favor that allowed me to be who I am today. God looks beyond my faults and provides me with everything I need through his grace and mercy.

As a church, we are putting the words to that song into action. We are extending the grace of God to children. The people in our church believe strongly in this mission. One family adopted five sisters in a single day. Because of the grace that has been extended to each one of us, we see this mission as a direct service to God. We adopt children out of love and obedience to him. Our mission has now spread across the entire nation.

I believe it is God's will that all children be raised in loving and kind environments. I also believe that the church has been commissioned to save a generation of children. The children being adopted are among the most underprivileged and neglected children across Texas.

Not only have we adopted and shared our vision with our congregation, we have now taken the message beyond our church walls. We share the same hope and joy we have experienced while telling others about the importance and the need for adoption.

Even though adoption is something we chose to do, sometimes it is full of unsuspected surprises. We have experienced all kinds of problems. Many difficulties stem from the children's previous home life. Many of them were beaten, molested or starved before they came to us.

We set high goals for ourselves. The arrival of 70 new children has been quite overwhelming. Eventually, we will have to build a new building to accommodate for the growth.

I continue to tell my congregation, "We are not here just to save souls. We are here to save lives." We have a great deal of work ahead for us. We are committed, however. We have been given patience and the gift of love. We believe these children are entitled to a productive life.

One of the greatest things we can do is to open our hearts and share our lives with these children. We want them to have a chance for bright and happy futures.

W.C. MARTIN

Reverend Martin and his wife reside in Possum Trot, Texas, with their children. Their church community provides foster care for seventy children and adopted more than sixty. The Martins share a miracle of love in their small East Texas town.

WORD OF GOD ∫PEAK

// PERFORMED BY MERCY ME //

I'm finding myself at a loss for words
And the funny thing is it's okay
The last thing I need is to be heard
But to hear what you would say

Chorus:
Word of God speak
Would you pour down like rain
Washing my eyes to see
Your majesty
To be still and know
That you're in this place
Please let me stay and rest
In Your holiness
Word of God speak

I'm finding myself in the midst of you
Beyond the music, beyond the noise
All that I need is to be with you
And in the quiet hear Your voice

Chorus

I'm finding myself at a loss for words
And the funny thing is it's okay"

/// HEARING GOD ƒPEAK ///

LAURA B.

y husband and I tried for five years to have a baby. While trying to conceive, we went through many ups and downs. I am currently leading a women's support group in my home for women who have had similar experiences. My husband and I are also expecting our first child.

We were married in the fall of 1994. We lived in Arizona for a year and a half. In 1996, we returned to my hometown, Cincinnati. I got a job in advertising with a major magazine. I saw an article introducing a new church, which met in a school in Hyde Park. The church was not far from our house.

Even though we had both grown up in church, for some reason, we were drawn to this seeker-oriented church that was geared toward reaching the un-churched.

A few years later, we decided it was time to start a family. It obviously wasn't in God's plan, however. During the next five years, I tried to get pregnant. I was not able to conceive. I worked with doctors and specialists and underwent many tests to determine the reasons for my infertility. Later, I was diagnosed with several medical problems, including Graves' disease and endometriosis. I received treatment and also underwent several outpatient procedures.

It was during those rough times that our faith was tested. Through everything, we clung to our faith. We learned what it meant to totally trust God. My faith grew by leaps and bounds and our marriage continued to grow stronger.

One verse from Jeremiah 29:11-14, helped me keep my focus and gave me hope: "'For I know the plans I have for you,' says the Lord. 'They are plans for good and not for disaster, to give you a future and a hope. In those days when you pray, I will listen. If you look for me in earnest, you will find me when you seek me. I will be found by you,' says the Lord."

We continued to seek God's will. We, oftentimes, asked him if it was in his will for us to have a baby. We joined Resolve, a support group for people with infertility problems. This group was not affiliated with a church, however. I became frustrated. They discouraged me from bringing up questions or concerns, which related infertility to God's will.

In the process, we considered in vitro fertilization (IVF). We sought to find out more about it and also to see if it was an option for us. We went to our pastor at Crossroads Community Church for guidance. We decided IVF was an option for us because the procedure involved a loving, married couple.

We discussed the story of Abraham and Sarah's desire to have a child and God's promise to them. We talked about Abraham and Sarah's impulsiveness and their lack of faith, which resulted in Abraham going outside the marriage to have a child. Then we talked about the blessing of Isaac, their biological child.

Going through this process made me realize there is a need for a Christian woman's group experiencing infertility.

A man in our church who had started a similar support group for divorced people once said that if a person sees a need for a group and there isn't one, maybe they should start it. He said we shouldn't wait for someone else to start it. His words obviously planted a seed in my mind.

I never felt like I could be a leader, but at that time, I wondered if God wanted me to start a group for infertile women. I began to have a feeling God was indeed talking to me. The feeling kept getting stronger and stronger. We had planned on doing an IVF cycle in July 2003. I debated starting a group at a time when I could become pregnant.

"God wouldn't have me start something I cannot finish," I thought foolishly. In the back of my mind, however, I still felt that God might truly be speaking to me and that this indeed might be his plan and purpose for my life.

I talked to God many times on my way to work. One morning, after another heartbreaking month, and another unsuccessful cycle, I pleaded with God to give me a sign to let me know whether or not he was going to grant my desire for a child. I felt that I needed an answer. If his answer was "no," I asked him to take the desire from me. If it was "yes," then I prayed he would use this journey to help me learn to trust him by turning everything over to him.

Within an hour after asking God to give me insight into his will for us, a client who had also struggled with infertility called me out of the blue. He felt God had told him to tell me that I would be blessed with a baby.

In July of 2003, we went ahead with IVF. It was unsuccessful. I felt like I had hit rock bottom and that God had deserted me.

The nagging feeling came back, even stronger, about starting the support group. I once again prayed to God in my car on the way to work. I begged him to speak to me and to tell me what he wanted me to do. Did he want me to start this group? Did he know the amount of pain and sadness that I was feeling at that moment?

I played the song "Word of God Speak" by Mercy Me over and over again in my car. The entire time I begged God to speak to me. I listened to the words of the song. "Word of God speak, won't you pour down like rain, washing my eyes to see your majesty."

I listened closely to the words of the song. I tried desperately to hear what God had to say, but heard nothing. I played the song again, got very quiet, and tried desperately to listen. Once again, nothing happened. Then I cried out to God, "Please God! Speak to me! Tell me what you want me to do! Do you want me to start this support group? I don't hear you, God! How can I listen to you? How do I know it's you?"

I pleaded with God five or six times, to no avail. Finally, after about a half an hour, I heard the line in the song, "won't you pour down like rain." I spoke to God in a kidding tone, "I just can't hear you! I need you to write it in the sky or have someone call me on my cell phone, or just put some rain on my windshield or something that I can see or hear!"

I played the song again, got quiet again, and at the exact time that the words of the song said "And in the quiet, I hear your voice," I saw the first drop of rain. In a matter of seconds, my entire windshield was covered in tiny droplets of rain. I cried and shook and turned on my windshield wipers. I looked out the window on both sides and all around me. I noticed that no one else had their windshield wipers turned on. The sun was shining brightly.

"You heard me," I cried. "You heard me! You're really there! Ok God! I'll do it! I'll do it!" When I parked my car, I just sat in the garage, shaking, crying, praying, and rejoicing. The next day, I called the church and told the pastor that God told me to start this support group. I asked for guidance on how I should get started.

Within one month, I had formed a group of seven women. We began meeting at each other's homes. Every woman who joined told me the group was an answer to a prayer.

Later, our pastor asked us to share our story before 1,200 people at an upcoming event at our church. As a result, our infertility support group grew from seven to seventeen women.

As of October 2004, nearly all of the original seven are either pregnant, in the process of adopting, or are already the proud parents of adopted children!

In June of 2004, I underwent the second IVF cycle. While waiting to see if the embryo would implant, a friend who had no idea I had just undergone IVF called me to tell me that she felt God had told her to call me and give her reassurance that he would bless me with a baby. He also told her to tell me that this blessing was from him alone, and had nothing to do with anything that my husband and I had done to make this happen. Not the IVF. Not the doctors. Not the special diet or the acupuncture. God alone was responsible.

Within one week after that phone call, I discovered that the baby had indeed implanted and I was pregnant for the first time. So in July of 2004, my husband and I were expecting.

By going through these experiences, we learned to listen to God's calling in our lives. We also learned to trust God completely and remain faithful in every situation. Most importantly, we learned how to obey him when he speaks to us.

LAURA B.

Laura is a senior account executive for a Cincinnati magazine. Laura is currently leading a Christian-based support group for other women who have been struggling with infertility.